Hartman – Koester Ancestry

This book introduces the American history of my Hartman and Koester In-Laws, and consists primarily of a collected set of papers, with some updates and corrections, that I wrote while researching the family of my Koester son-in-law's mother, Margaret Hartman Koester.

The intent is to preserve this research as part of the collection of books I have written concerning my own ancestry which, by extension, is also part of the ancestry of my Koester grandsons.

Also included in this book is a short introduction to my grandsons' Koester ancestry, as well as a reproduction of a privately printed "Koster Family Album" in the possession of my Koester son-in-law's family. The album was originally prepared in Germany (and in German) in 1928, updated and translated to English in 1943, and updated for the 1971 printing that is reproduced here.

Frank Oberle

Hartman – Koester Ancestry

Portions initially created 2009 by Frank Oberle
Revised June 2016

Cover Painting: Watercolor by my first cousin JoAnn Iglehart

ISBN-13: 978-0692665350
ISBN-10: 0692665358

(Engenthal Press)

Preface

As intimated on the cover leaf, this small book is primarily for my Koester grandsons to complement the books about my own family history should they ever decide to explore their genealogy. It was their own mother, after all, who gave me the genealogy "bug," and wandered around with me to various town halls and countless cemeteries in several countries and states in search of our ancestors. Two of my other children and a few grandchildren even visited the Oberle Hotel and Restaurant in Kilstett in Alsace with us.

Such research can be both addictive and fun; hopefully these materials can help one of my grandsons who might ever decide to undertake further research. Other books I've written that are relevant to my Koester grandsons include:

    The Oberle Family ISBN-13: 978-061595529-2
    Our Gonce Ancestors ISBN-13: 978-061592314-7
    Doctor Abraham Rudolph Gonce – Missouri Pioneer...ISBN-13: 978-061591244-8
    Our Hulshoff & Kerchner Ancestors............................ISBN-13: 978-069265057-8

Scope

The discussion of my grandsons' Hartman ancestry consists of sections for each of the lines leading to their paternal grandmother's direct line, including the Caruth, Griffin, and Hunt families, along with charts for each. Because there still needs to be more research on each line before looking across the Atlantic for records in their various countries-of-origin, I have limited the discussions of each family to their arrival and lives in this country, including their dates and places of arrival if I could locate that information. At the end of each section, I've listed some suggestions for further research that could still be done in this country should anyone feel so inclined.

A diagram of the Hartman lineage in the form of an ancestral chart with traditional German Ahnentafel numbering[1] is provided on page 17 to show the general scope of what is discussed in each section.

The original papers which have been adapted for this book were addressed to my grandsons' Koester-side grandmother Margaret, leading to frequent use of the terms "you," "your" and the like. I have left these terms mostly unaltered. Likewise I have left the original Ahnentafel numbers intact in the narrative.

Various handwritten notes (clues) written by Margaret and provided to me when I was doing this research are scattered throughout the discussions.

The first of two sections relating to the Koester family's history is a short summary of my grandsons' direct lineage along with copies of some interesting documents regarding that history. The second is a reproduction of the aforementioned "Koster Family Album."

---

[1] This term is explained in the section "Ahnentafel Numbers" below.

Ahnentafel Numbers

The Ahnentafel (literally, "Ancestor Table") numbering scheme was developed by German genealogists to permit easy identification of particular ancestors in an ancestry tree relative to the person at the root of the tree. Essentially, this root person (in the chart on page 17, for instance, my grandsons' paternal grandmother Margaret) has been assigned the arbitrary number a1. Her father would then be number a2 (her number 1 multiplied by 2), and her mother would be number a3 (her father's number plus 1). In the chart, therefore Margaret appears at the lowest (root) point with the "a1" designator, and her parents immediately above with the "a2" and "a3" designators.

Margaret's paternal grandparents would be a4 (2 x 2) and a5 (4 + 1), and her maternal grandparents would be a6 (3 x 2) and a7 (6 + 1) and so forth. Her four pairs of great-grandparents are therefore 8 & 9, 10 & 11, 12 & 13, and 14 & 15. Anyone's father can be found by doubling his or her Ahnentafel number and adding 1 to that to obtain their mother's number.

Because this book is ultimately intended for my Koester grandsons, It would be useful to adjust the Ahnentafel numbers to show one of them as the "a1" root; this wasn't done for several reasons:

1. For privacy reasons, genealogy publications generally avoid discussing and even mentioning living people who are below a certain age (typically 72).
2. Reconstructing the charts would have required more work than I cared to do.
3. Calculating the Ahnentafel numbers for the charts in this book with respect to my grandsons (i.e. with one of them as the "a1" root) will provide a useful mathematical exercise for those grandsons who believe they are math smarties.

   As a hint, my grandsons' paternal grandmother Margaret would appear in such a chart as "a5" and I would be "a6" even though I would not appear on any chart in this book. For confirmation, Ahnentafel numbers on the ancestry charts on pages 46 (Hartman), 64 (Caruth), 102 (Hunt), and 131 (Koester) are given with reference to my grandsons.

Abbreviations

These are primarily used when documenting the source of particular census pages such as the one on page 22. This example is a copy of a form filled out during the very first United States Census taken in 1790. In the caption, which reads "1790 Census: John Hartman Household in Hereford Twp, Berks Cty, Pa," showing John Hartman's Household in Hereford Township (abbreviated Twp) in Berks County (abbreviated Cty), Pennsylvania. The standard two letter abbreviations adopted by the U.S. Postal service are used for states (e.g. Pa for Pennsylvania), but only the abbreviation for Illinois is capitalized for clarity. "Hhd" is sometimes used in the same context to abbreviate "household."

Table of Contents

PREFACE..III
   Scope..iii
   Ahnentafel Numbers...iv
   Abbreviations..iv
   The Hartman Family, circa 1945...viii

HARTMAN ANCESTRY..1
   Origins..1
   Your Ancestors...3
   George Hartman..4
      Hartman Residences in the 19th Century..4
   Children of George Hartman and his Wife..4
   Children of Phillip and Elizabeth Hartman..6
   Children of George and Margaret Fox Hartman..7
   Children of Samuel W. and Rachel Anna Breece Hartman.....................................8
   Cynthia (Caruth) and Grier Hartman..10
   Children of Samuel Grier and Cynthia Caruth Hartman.......................................10
   Ray Ellis Hartman..12
   "Miss Frances Griffin of Shabbona Grove"...13
   Suggestions for Further Research..14
      Location of the Palatinate...14
   Ray Ellis and Frances Genevieve (Griffin) Hartman..17
   Ahnentafel Chart for Margaret Hartman Koester...18
   Hartman Ancestry Diagram 1 of 4 for Margaret Hartman Koester.....................19
   Hartman Ancestry Diagram 2 of 4 for Margaret Hartman Koester.....................20
   Hartman Ancestry Diagram 3 of 4 for Margaret Hartman Koester.....................21
   Hartman Ancestry Diagram 4 of 4 for Margaret Hartman Koester (Hartman-Caruth)........22
   1790 Census: John Hartman Household in Hereford Twp, Berks Cty, Pa..........23
   1790-1840 Census Transcriptions: Phillip and George Hartman Households....24
   1790 Census: Phillip Hartman Household in Cocalico Twp, Lancaster Cty, Pa.25
   1800 Census: Phillip Hartman Household: Greenwood Twp, Northumberland Cty, Pa......26
   1810 Census: Phl Hartman Household in Mahoning Twp, Northumberland Cty, Pa..........27
   1820 Census: Phillip Hartman Household in Mahoning Twp, Columbia Cty Pa.28
   1840 Census: Phillip & George Hartman Households in Hemlock Twp, Columbia Cty, Pa. 29
   1850 Census: George Hartman Household in Hemlock Twp, Columbia Cty, Pa............30
   1850 Census: William Cox Hhd in Hemlock Twp, Columbia Cty, Pa; w/Samuel Hartman..31
   1860 Census: George & Samuel Hartman Households in Hemlock Twp, Columbia Cty, Pa 32
   1870 Census: Amos Hartman Household (w/George) in Hemlock Twp, Columbia Cty, Pa. 33
   1870 Census: Samuel Hartman Households in West Hemlock Twp, Montour Cty, Pa......34
   1880 Census: Samuel Hartman Household in West Hemlock Twp, Montour Cty, Pa.......35
   1900 Census: James Bredbender (?) Household in Center Twp, Columbia County, Pa....36
   1900 Census: Grier Hartman Household in Paw Paw Twp, DeKalb County, IL..............37
   1910 Census: Grier Hartman Household in Paw Paw Twp, DeKalb County, IL..............38
   12 September 1918 U.S. Draft Registration Card for Ray Ellis Hartman............39

    5 June 1917 U.S. Draft Registration Card for Stearl J. Hartman..............................39
    12 September 1918 U.S. Draft Registration Card for Dale Caruth Hartman......................40
    5 June 1917 U.S. Draft Registration Card for Arthur C. Hartman...........................40
    5 June 1917 U.S. Draft Registration Card for Russell Hartman..............................41
    1920 Census: Grier Hartman Household in Paw Paw Twp, DeKalb County, IL................42
    1930 Census: Grier Hartman Household in Paw Paw Twp, DeKalb County, IL................43
    1930 Census: Ray Hartman Household in Shalbona Twp, DeKalb County, IL................44
    1940 Census: Cynthia Hartman in Earlville, LaSalle County; IL...........................45
    1940 Census: Ray Hartman Household in Clinton Twp, DeKalb County, IL................46
    My Grandsons' Hartman-side Ahnentafel Chart..47

CARUTH ANCESTRY..48

    Andrew Caruth (1807-1889)..48
    Jennie Herbertson Caruth (1808-1884)..48
    Children of Andrew and Jennie Herbertson Caruth..49
    Alexander Caruth (May 1830 – Aug 1881)...50
    The McCarrells..51
    Children of Alexander and Mary Jane McCarrell Caruth.....................................52
    Alexander and Mary Jane McCarrell Caruth...52
    Suggestions for Further Research..53
    Caruth Ancestry Diagram 1 of 1 for Margaret Hartman Koester............................55
    May 1848 – An early "Passenger Bill of Rights" giving an idea of shipboard conditions......56
    12 September 1853 Passenger Manifest of the Enterprise: Liverpool to New York...........57
    12 September 1853 Passenger Manifest of the Enterprise: Liverpool to New York...........58
    1870 Census: Andrew Caruth Household in Paw Paw Twp, Lee County, IL................59
    1870 Census: Andrew Caruth Household in Paw Paw Twp, Lee County, IL................60
    1870 Census: Alexander Caruth Household in Brooklyn Twp, Lee Cty, IL................61
    1880 Census: Andrew Caruth Household in Wyoming Twp, Lee County, IL................62
    1880 Census: Alexander Caruth Household in Wyoming Twp, Lee Cty, IL................63
    1900 Census: Thomas A. Caruth (w/Mary J. Caruth) Hhd in Wyoming Twp, Lee Cty, IL..64
    My Grandsons' Caruth-side Ahnentafel Chart..65

GRIFFIN ANCESTRY..66

    Immigration..67
    The Children of Patrick and Mary Ann Grady Griffin.......................................69
    The Griffin's Origins Revisited..70
    The Family Farm..71
    Edward F. Griffin, circa 1898...71
    Your Grandfather Edward's Date of Death..72
    Griffin Tombstone at St. James Cemetery in Lee..72
    The Children of Ed and Maggie Hunt Griffin..73
    Maggie Hunt Griffin, circa 1898...73
    Suggestions for Further Research..74
    Griffin Ancestry Diagram 1 of 2 for Margaret Hartman Koester............................76
    Griffin Ancestry Diagram 2 of 2 for Margaret Hartman Koester (Griffin-Hunt)............77
    1 June 1857 Passenger Manifest of the Lady Russell: Liverpool to New York..............78
    1 June 1857 Passenger Manifest of the Lady Russell: Liverpool to New York..............79
    2 June 1857 Passenger Manifest (cover) of Meridian: Liverpool to Boston;................80
    2 June 1857 Passenger Manifest of Meridian: Liverpool to Boston........................81
    1870 Census: Patrick Griffin Household in Clinton Twp, DeKalb County, IL..............82
    1880 Census: Patrick Griffin Household in Clinton Twp, DeKalb Cty, IL.................83

1900 Census: Edward & Patrick Griffin Households in Clinton Twp, DeKalb Cty, IL..........84
1910 Census: Edward Griffin Household in Clinton Twp, DeKalb Cty, IL..........................85
1920 Census: Edward Griffin Household in Clinton Twp, DeKalb Cty, IL..........................86
1930 Census: Edward Griffin Household in Clinton Twp, DeKalb Cty, IL..........................87

HUNT ANCESTRY..........89

The Dreishmeyer Family..........90
The Children of Thomas and Etta Dreishmeyer Hunt..........90
Iowa Counties..........91
Maggie (Hunt) Griffin..........92
Suggestions for Further Research..........92
Hunt Ancestry Diagram 1 of 1 for Margaret Hartman Koester..........94
25 Oct 1847 Passenger Arrival Manifest of "Bremen Ship Emma" (1)..........95
25 Oct 1847 Passenger Arrival Manifest of "Bremen Ship Emma" (2)..........96
28 May 1862 Passenger Arrival Manifest of the Neptune..........97
1870 Census: Margaret Hunt Hhd (w/Thomas & Etta) in Northville Twp, LaSalle Cty, IL.98
1880 Census: Thomas Hunt Household in Somanauk Twp, DeKalb Cty, IL..........99
1900 Census: Thomas Hunt Household in Cedar Twp, Greene Cty, Ia..........100
1900 Census: Thomas Hunt Household in Cedar Twp, Greene Cty, Ia;..........101
1910 Census: Thomas Hunt Household in Highland Twp, Greene Cty, Ia..........102
1920 Census: Etta Hunt Household in Vinton Twp, Benton Cty, Ia;..........103
My Grandsons' Hunt & Griffin-side Ahnentafel Chart..........104

KOESTER ANCESTRY..........105

The Koester Name and Family..........105
A Brief History of the Koester Line..........107
Johann Johannsen Kuster $^{ID\ 1328}$ and his unknown Wife..........107
Johann Johannsen Kuster $^{ID\ 1332}$ and Maria Henrichs $^{ID\ 1333}$..........107
Johann Johannsen Kuster $^{ID\ 1334}$ and Metke Hermanns Bose $^{ID\ 1337}$..........107
Otto Johannsen Kuster $^{ID\ 1343}$ and Wobke Gerdes $^{ID\ 1347}$..........107
Herman Johan Kuster $^{ID\ 1361}$ and Minelt Gerdes $^{ID\ 1366}$..........108
Otte Janssen Kuster $^{ID\ 1305}$ and Anna Katherina Osterkamp $^{ID\ 1306}$..........108
Folkert Otten Koester $^{ID\ 1302}$ and Memarich Sanders $^{ID\ 1390}$..........108
Boike Anton Koester $^{ID\ 678}$ and Ida Bruns $^{ID\ 679}$..........109
The S.S. Grosser Kurfürst..........109
Ida Annette Bruns at age 18..........111
Anton and Ida Koester in 1938..........111
Anton, Wes, and Ida Koester in 1940..........112
Map of North Sea Coast showing the Koester family's European Ancestral Areas..........114
Bruns Ancestry Diagram 1 of 1 for Wesley Koester..........115
Koester Ancestry Diagram 4 of 5 for Wesley Koester..........116
9 May 1884 Passenger Manifest for the S.S. Oder; pg 1..........117
9 May 1884 Passenger Manifest for the S.S. Oder; pg 2..........118
11 May 1909 Passenger Manifest for the S.S. Kronprinzessin Cecilie; left side..........119
11 May 1909 Passenger Manifest for the S.S. Kronprinzessin Cecilie; right side..........120
1910 U.S. Census showing Anton Koester in Grant Twp, Plymouth Cty, Ia..........121
3 June 1914 Passenger Manifest for the S.S. Grosser Kurfürst; left side..........122
3 June 1914 Passenger Manifest for the S.S. Grosser Kurfürst; right side..........123
12 September 1918: World War I Draft Card for Anton Boicke Koester..........124
29 April 1923 Passenger Manifest for the S.S. President Fillmore..........125
6 August 1923 Passenger Manifest for the S.S. President Fillmore; left side..........126

6 August 1923 Passenger Manifest for the S.S. President Fillmore; right side....................127
1930 U.S.Census showing Anton Koester family in Jordan Twp, Whiteside Cty, IL..........128
1940 U.S. Census showing Anton Koester's family in Palmyra Twp, Lee Cty, IL...............129
1940 U.S. Census showing Anton Koester's family in Palmyra Twp, Lee Cty, IL...............130
Family History Notes from Wesley Koester's Scrapbook; page 1.......................................131
Family History Notes from Wesley Koester's Scrapbook; page 5.......................................132
My Grandsons' Koester-side Ahnentafel Chart..133

THE KOSTER FAMILY ALBUM..135

The Hartman Family, circa 1945
Top row, left-to-right: Raymond (Bud); Genevieve; Donald
Bottom row, left-to-right: Beverly; Father Ray; Mother Frances; Margaret

Hartman Ancestry

A diagram of your direct lineage in the form of a traditional German Ahnentafel Chart is provided on page 17 to show the general context.

Origins

Eastern Pennsylvania

Hartman Households by County in the 1790 Census

We know from the 1790 Census that, at the end of the eighteenth century, there were Hartman households in various counties of eastern Pennsylvania, most notably Berks, Northampton, and York. The number of these households in each county is shown in red on the map to the right. Your ancestors can be definitively traced back to the original Northumberland County, shown as the white-bordered area on the map, although they could not have settled there until 1781 at the earliest[2]. Your family lived in the portion that later became Columbia County from some time following the American Revolutionary War to the present, and many of their descendants are still living in Columbia and Montour counties.

One observation I made while looking through arrival records[3] was that the name "Hartma<u>n</u>" seemed to be the predominant, though not exclusive, form of the spelling for those whose arrivals are documented from Colonial times through the 1820s, and that they almost always arrived at the port of Philadelphia. The "Hartma<u>nn</u>" spelling likewise dominated the arrivals in the middle and late decades of the nineteenth century; these Hartma<u>nn</u>s typically arrived in New York.

---

[2] The reason for this will be explained later.
[3] Arrival records consist of records like passenger manifests (scarce in the period the Hartmans arrived, but useful for your other lines), baggage lists (to provide import duty exemptions for colonial immigrants), published indexes derived from various sources, and web sites from Ellis Island, Castle Garden, and the like. Early churches often recorded new arrivals in their meeting records that can be useful if a specific location and denomination can be identified, but I wasn't able to find any of them to review.

To provide some background: Up until 1749, the representatives of Penn's colony had been making regular purchases of land from the local Indians in what is now Luzerne and eastern Columbia Counties. In 1754, Connecticut also purchased land in this same area from the Indians. Interestingly, the Indian's concept of land ownership being quite different from that of the Europeans, both groups ended up believing they were sole owners of the same large section of land in what is now northeastern Pennsylvania. Ownership and settlement rights in the areas in the east of Northumberland County as well as the whole of Luzerne and Lackawanna Counties came to be strongly disputed – not, as might be imagined, by the French and the English, or the English and the Indians, but between Connecticut and Pennsylvania.

Before any of this was settled, however, both groups came to be driven out of what is now Columbia County in 1763 by the Indian raids that followed General Braddock's defeat in the French and Indian War. Even before that time the area was considered the far western frontier, and conditions were hardly improved by 1768, when the Indians were quelled and the area could again be safely settled.

It was likely around twenty years later that the first of your Hartman ancestors came to the area. The historical record shows that the initial settlers were Quakers from Ireland, followed by Dutch, Welsh, Germans, and Scotch-Irish. According to the histories of the area, most of the German settlers, who began arriving in about 1788, came from Berks County. There is other, more specific, information to suggest that your own ancestors first lived in Berks County – but more about that later.

At the time, Columbia County was a difficult place to reach as well as a difficult place to live. No roads existed at the time, and the primary means of transporting household belongings was the packhorse; even wagons were not practical, meaning that the quantity of provisions a settler could bring was quite limited. Log homes were constructed by hand, and these needed to be built quite quickly in order to prepare for the Pennsylvania winters. This was only a land of opportunity for those with keen eyesight!

If you are interested in reading more about the history and conditions in this area of Pennsylvania during the colonial period and nineteenth century, the Pennsylvania State University Library has a copy of "Historical and Biographical Annals of Columbia and Montour Counties, Pennsylvania," which is on-line at: https://secureapps.libraries.psu.edu/digitalbookshelf/bookindex.cfm?oclc=30629788. The Columbia County Historical and Genealogical Society also has a web site with some interesting information at www.colcohist-gensoc.org/

Your Ancestors

For various reasons, I was unable to definitively track your direct line further back than your great-great-great-grandfather[4] Phillip Hartman, who lived from somewhere between 1761 and 1766 to sometime in the 1840s. In the information I've collected, there is undoubtedly data about Phillip's siblings, and possibly his parents, but there isn't enough detail to prove the exact relationships among the names I've identified. There is sufficient circumstantial information, however, to guess that Phillip is probably the son of George Hartman[5], discussed below, and that he had at least two older brothers and an older sister.

It would be far more speculative to guess who your 5th great-grandfather might be, since I've been unable to locate any local Pennsylvania census or tax records prior to the American Revolution that might provide a clue. There are several likely candidates:

- Fredrick Hartman[6] arrived with his family and appeared in the Philadelphia Courthouse on 11 August 1732 as part of a group of 106 Palatinate (called Pfalz in German) immigrant families arriving from London on the ship Samuel to take their oath of allegiance in order to settle in Penn's colony. With their families, this group as a whole represented 279 persons. See the map on page 14.
- Laurens Hartman[7] likewise appeared before the same court as part of another group of 112 Palatine heads-of-household on 19 September of the same year. He arrived on the ship Johnson from London as part of a total group of 330 people.
- Ulrich Hartman[8] arrived with his family in Philadelphia 25 November 1740 on the ship Loyal Judith from Landsberg, Zweibruecken in the Palatinate. Ulrich is possibly your early ancestor, but that can't be proven.

These were the only Hartman immigrants I could locate in the Colonial period, so any of these might be your ancestor, but there is no evidence to say that any of them actually is. Knowing that all these arrived from the Palatinate, however, suggests that your ancestors, whoever they were, were likely also Palatines.

---

[4] The form "3rd great-grandfather" will be used in the remainder of this book.
[5] Tracing your grandfather's ancestry back demonstrates that at least four generations of his ancestors lived in the same area. Because the number of Hartmans listed in the censuses of that area steadily declines from 1880 to 1790, there is a clear indication that most (but not all) of your ancestors descended from the earliest of these.
[6] Pennsylvania German Immigrants 1709-1786; Don Yoder, ed.; ISBN 0-8063-0892-3; LoC 80-50502
[7] ibid.
[8] Ship Passenger Lists – Pennsylvania and Delaware (1641-1825); Carl Boyer; ISBN 0-936124-02-4; LoC 79-57204

George Hartman

In the first United States Census, taken in 1790, William Hartman was the only household in Northumberland County recorded with your surname, and he lived in Greenwood Township (see the map to the right). Because his is the earliest name to appear, it might be tempting to assume that he is the first of your direct ancestors, but I don't believe this is the case. I was unable to locate William in 1800, but he appears again in later years, so he didn't die before then. Phillip Hartman first appears in the 1800 census, as do John and George Hartman.

Several things are clear from examining these records.

William, John and Phillip continue to appear in the subsequent census records, but George does not. He could therefore be a much older sibling of the other three, but I suspect it is more likely that he is their father. Assuming that my guess is correct, George would therefore be your 4th great-grandfather [a64]. He was likely born between 1725 and 1730 and, of course, certainly before 1755.

Hartman Residences in the 19th Century
Greenwood Township (Green)
Hemlock Township (Violet)
Mahoning Township (Blue)

Compare to the previous map.

Professions weren't listed in the census until 1850, but we can assume from the history of the area that George, Phillip, and the others were most likely to have been farmers since, at the time, there was really no other practical full-time profession in the area. Even after coal began to become important in nearby areas, later generations of your Hartman ancestors mostly seem to have been farmers, so this seems like a reasonable guess. Being pioneers, of course, the earlier settlers also served as their own architects, builders, blacksmiths, hunters, and whatever else was required. Their wives served as teachers, seamstresses, nurses and housewives as well as farmers.

Children of George Hartman and his Wife

If George was indeed your 4th great-grandfather, he must have married in about 1748. To continue the speculation, there were at least the three sons mentioned:

- William was likely the oldest, since the age groupings into which he fell in later censuses narrow down his year of birth to somewhere between 1741 and 1750.

- Phillip, your direct ancestor, was likely the youngest, since later censuses indicate that he must have been born between 1761 and 1766. He will be discussed below.
- Somewhere in the middle is John Hartman, who was born in Berks County in November of 1757. On 9 January 1833, while living in Hemlock Township, John applied for and received a pension for his service in the Revolutionary War. He was originally drafted on 1 August 1776 (less than a month after the Declaration of Independence) into Captain Ludwig's Militia in Bucks County, where he was living at the time, and served his required three months. He remained in the militia for another term as a substitute[9] for Joseph Marchant. John primarily served in Amboy and Staten Island. After leaving the militia, he returned to live in Berks County. This would tend to reinforce the notion that your Hartman ancestors lived in Berks County prior to the Revolutionary War. I was only able to obtain very low resolution copies of his pension application of 1833, so these segments have not been reproduced here. It is worth noting, however, that John's pension application was "marked" rather than signed, indicating that John, like most people at that time, was not literate. John appeared in the 1790 census (see page 22) living in Hereford Township in Berks County.

From 1800 through his death in late 1840, John continued to live in Columbia County.

Additionally, it seems reasonable to believe that George Hartman and his wife had other children:

- Francis Hartman's household was immediately next to John's in 1790, making it likely that he was related, but I have been unable to locate any other trace of him. My guess is that he is another son of George's, but the possibility that he was actually the father, and George an older brother of the others, should be kept in mind.
- Assuming George was the father, and that he was born in about 1725-1730 (all we know for sure is that he was born prior to 1755), the single female listed as living with him in the 1800 census could not have been his wife, but was likely a daughter.

If we assume that the female in the 1800 census was a daughter, we can further speculate that George's wife (and your 4th great-grandmother) must have died before 1800. George doesn't appear in any census after 1800, nor is there any unexplained older male in one of his descendants' households in later censuses. This would imply that he likely died sometime before 1810; he may be the

---

[9] At the time, a draftee was permitted to pay someone to serve in his place.

George Hartman who died in 1803 and is buried in the Union Cemetery in Boyertown, Berks County, Pennsylvania (see the map on page 1).

Page 18 shows a family diagram taken from the set alluded to earlier, and shows the earliest generation of your Hartman ancestry that is supported by enough circumstantial evidence to be defensible. From this point on, there is adequate extant documentation to minimize the need for inference and speculation.

Children of Phillip and Elizabeth Hartman

Phillip and his wife Elizabeth seem to have been married sometime in 1787 or 1788, and eventually had at least seven children. The fourth of the Hartman family diagrams, reproduced on page 19, shows their family makeup. By 1800[10], the census shows that they were living in Greenwood Township (see the earlier map), and had four daughters and one son, who we can determine is your 2nd great-grandfather George Hartman. A copy of the census form is shown on page 25; because these early censuses were mostly sheets of paper with hand-drawn columns that lacked titles, tables are provided on page 23 to show how the numbers on the sheets relate to the requested age categories for each census year.

By 1810 (see the previously referenced table; a reproduction of the census form is on page 26 for comparison), Phillip and his wife had moved southwest to nearby Mahoning Township and added two more sons. Although Mahoning is shown in Montour County in the map above, the town was still part of Northumberland County in 1810. Phillip's family structure is outlined in the diagram on page 18.

During the next decade, the population of the area grew sufficiently that Northumberland County was subdivided, with Columbia County being split off on March 22, 1813; Montour County was created some years later. In 1820, Mahoning Township was part of Columbia County.

We can tell from that year's census (see page 27) that Phillip's two oldest daughters were no longer living in the household, and I believe the evidence suggests that one of the two remaining females was not Phillip's daughter, but the wife of his oldest son George.

---

[10] A copy of the 1790 census for someone named Phillip Hartman is shown on page 24 but, because he is located in Lancaster County, I am fairly certain this is *not* the same person as your 3rd great-grandfather.

George, who is your 2nd great-grandfather, was certainly married to Margaret Fox by this time and, since he doesn't appear in a household of his own, it seems reasonable to assume that he was still living on his father's farm.

Another male between the ages of 18 and 26 appears in Phillip's household in 1820; since he would have appeared in the earlier censuses if he were a son, he was likely a farmhand.

Note on the census form that the neighboring household at this time is that of William Hartman, born between 1781 and 1790; this is likely the oldest son of Phillip's brother William.

I haven't been able to locate 1830 census records for many of the Hartmans in this area, leading to a suspicion that some records may have been lost, but I can't find any reference stating that as a fact.

By 1840 (see page 28), Phillip and his wife Elizabeth, each now over seventy years old, were living in Hemlock Township, slightly northeast of their previous home (see the map on page 4). What is interesting is that there were now two additional females in the household. The older of the two was somewhere between 20 and 29 years old, and the other between 15 and 19 – definitely too young to be their own children. One can speculate that they may have been live-in servants, or perhaps even their granddaughters[11] but, without having the 1830 census for comparison, it is impossible to tell for certain. They don't appear to be George and Margaret's children, however, since those are all accounted for in a separate household.

Elizabeth died after the census was taken, on 28 July 1840, while Phillip lived until 30 August 1846. Both are buried in the Columbia Hill Cemetery in Montour County.

Children of George and Margaret Fox Hartman

As mentioned earlier, I was unable to locate George and Margaret in the 1830 census for Columbia County. By the time of the 1840 census (see page 28) however, your 2nd great-grandfather George was now listed as a Head-of-Household in Hemlock Township, Columbia County. His property was listed as the household adjacent to his father Phillip's, from which we can infer that he had possibly either purchased or been given some or all of the family farm once his father became old enough to retire.

George and Margaret Fox, who was born in 1796, had been married in about 1817, and had a total of fifteen children – ten sons and three daughters; your

---

[11] If, for instance, a married daughter died during childbirth, her husband may have abandoned the household to find work elsewhere, leaving the children in their care.

great-grandfather Samuel Wesley Hartman was the ninth of these children, and was born in March 1831 in Columbia County. George's family structure is outlined with his father's in the diagram on page 18.

By the time of the 1850 census (see page 29), only the four youngest of their children were still living at home. Your great-grandfather Samuel had left home and moved to the nearby farm of William Cox by 1850 (see page 30, where he is listed as "Saml") to work as a farm hand; he was then 18 years old.

When the 1860 census was taken (see page 31), George's two youngest children Jacob and Margaret were the last of his offspring living at home. Amos, the next youngest son after your great-grandfather, was now 25 years old, and had left farming to set up shop as a blacksmith. He had gotten married shortly after the last census to a woman named Mahala and, by 1860, they had four children; Amos' real estate holdings in 1860[12] were listed as being worth $590.

Your 2nd great-grandmother Margaret died on 5 December 1861; by the time of the 1870 census (see page 33), her husband George had moved in with his son Amos and his family.

Your 2nd great-grandfather George died on 22 June 1876; he and Margaret are buried in the Columbia Hill Cemetery where his parents are buried.

Children of Samuel W. and Rachel Anna Breece Hartman

In about 1853, your great-grandfather Samuel married Rachel Anna Breece, who was born on 23 August 1829. The 1860 census (see page 31) lists her name as Rachael, while the 1870 census (see page 32) refers to her as Anna.

Samuel and his wife had eight children that I could locate, with three of them born by the time of the 1860 census (see page 37). Samuel's family structure is outlined in the diagram on page 19. At least four more children were born in the next decade, the last (seventh) of these being your grandfather Samuel Grier Hartman, who was born on 4 February 1868, although his age was listed as 5[13] for some reason. This is quite inconsistent with his age as recorded on the next six censuses (which are all consistent with the 1868 birth year), but there seems to be no doubt that this is your grandfather.

During the Civil War Samuel served briefly (from 3 Sep 1864 to 21 Jun 1865) in Company H, 15th Regiment, 160th Volunteers of the Pennsylvania Cavalry.

Anna died on 1 September 1877, and is buried in the Columbia Hill Cemetery. The 1880 census (see page 34) shows that Samuel was living in West Hemlock

---

[12] This 1860 census page, NARC m653, roll 1098, page 817, is not reproduced here.
[13] I tried to read it as a "2," which it should and may be, but it really looks like a "5."

Township, in Montour County with only his four youngest children – including your grandfather Samuel Grier Hartman, who was 11 years old at the time. His daughter (and your grandfather's older sister) Malvernia (called Nell), who was 16, had dropped out of school[14] and was "keeping house."

By 1900, your great-grandfather Samuel had moved in with his daughter Ellen and her husband James R. Bredbentley, and was living with them at the time of the 1900 census (see page 35 for an image of this census form). Samuel died on 21 June 1910, and is buried in Lime Ridge Evangelical United Brethren Cemetery in Lime Ridge, Columbia County, Pennsylvania. I was unable to determine why he doesn't seem to be buried with his wife.

In 1880, as mentioned above, your grandfather Samuel Grier Hartman was living with his widowed father in West Hemlock Township in Montour County, Pennsylvania. He was 11 years old at the time and, although he was listed in that census as a farm laborer, he was still attending school. It is difficult to say for certain but, given the history of the area in which he lived, it is quite likely that he was the first of your Hartman ancestors who was able to read and write.

In your letter (shown to the right), you indicated that he had come from Bloomsburg, Pennsylvania, which is the largest community in Columbia County and is located very near the current Interstate-80. Bloomsburg and Catawissa, which is a little southeast of Bloomsburg, were and are home to what appears to be quite a lot of your significant extended family. The only evidence I could locate to support his place of birth was his tombstone inscription. Since the 1890 census is missing, however, it seems reasonable to accept that he probably lived there prior to coming to Illinois. Bloomsburg was then and is now the Columbia County Seat.

We can set some bounds on the time period during which your grandfather might have lived there[15], though. It seems unlikely, although not unheard of, that he would have gone off on his own before the age of 16, which would have been sometime in 1885. He could, perhaps, have traveled with an older sibling, but I have been able to locate two of his older brothers, William and James, and they were still living in Columbia County, Pennsylvania as late as 1900.

Interestingly, however, it appears that the third son George, who was about ten years older than your grandfather, may have gone to Illinois in the late 1870s. There is no trace of a George W. Hartman in Pennsylvania in 1880, but a George W. Hartman, age 23 and born in Pennsylvania, was working as a farm laborer in Cornwall Township, Henry County, IL, for John and Ellenor (sic)

---

[14] This can be determined by the lack of a check mark in column 21 of the 1880 census form.
[15] This will be helpful if you decide to pursue his movements further.

Darin then. John and Ellenor indicated on the census that they had both come from Pennsylvania; their oldest daughter Mildred was born in Illinois in 1858, so they must have migrated before then. By the time of the 1900 census[16], this George had been married for sixteen years and had six children. In spite of the possible Pennsylvania connection, I was unable to locate John Darin in the 1850 census to see if he may have been a neighbor of George's father Samuel. So – there are no good clues in anything I looked at that would suggest why your grandfather came to Illinois.

Cynthia (Caruth) and Grier Hartman

We can speculate that he must have been in Illinois for long enough to meet and marry Cynthia Jacoby Caruth; their wedding took place there on 26 December 1890. Although this is speculative, it's a reasonable conclusion that your grandfather probably left Pennsylvania for Illinois some time between 1885 and 1889. Because the 1890 census was destroyed, it isn't clear whether he stayed with his older brother (if indeed the Illinois George W. Hartman was his brother) for any length of time, or simply set off for Illinois for other reasons.

You also mentioned in your letter to me that you thought your grandfather had been called "Grier." The census records for 1900 through 1930 all show the first name Grier (although the census takers didn't seem to spell that consistently), so that certainly seems to be the case.

Children of Samuel Grier and Cynthia Caruth Hartman

Your grandfather's wife Cynthia Caruth was born on 27 October 1865 in Illinois; her ancestors are discussed in "Caruth Ancestry" which begins on page 47.

Grier and Cynthia's family is diagrammed on page 21. Once married, they settled in Paw Paw Township, DeKalb County, and between early 1892 and 1908, they had at least eight children, of whom your father Ray Ellis was the fourth, born 21 March 1898.

---

[16] I didn't include an image of the census form in this book, since I'm not certain this is your grandfather's brother. The reference is National Archives Series t623, Roll 306, page 245. The names, ages, birth months and years, etc. of his wife and children are all easy to read.

The early growth of the family can be followed in the censuses of 1900 and 1910 (reproduced on pages 36 and 37); by that time, all of their children had been born, although the sixth died very young between 1900 and 1910[17]. The 1900 census, by the way, confirms Cynthia's month and year of birth as being in October 1865.

A Volunteer draws the first numbers in the United States Draft for World War I

The next decade brought the infamous assassination at Sarajevo and subsequent "War to end all Wars[18]." On 18 May 1917, the Selective Service Act was passed, which affected all males born between 1872 and 1899.

Since the Hartman's first five children were all sons, and all born between 1890 and 1901, each of them was required to register, although the dates varied because of their specific years of birth.

On June 5, 1917, your oldest uncles Arthur, Stearl (James) and Russell registered at the local draft board office in Sycamore.

---

[17] We know this because, on the columns 11 and 12 of the 1900 census (see page 36), Cynthia reports that she was the mother of 5 children, with 5 living), but on columns 10 and 11 of the 1910 census (page 37), she says that she is the mother of 8 with 7 living.

[18] ... and we know how successful that turned out to be ...

Your father and his younger brother Dale registered on 12 September 1918[19]. As a point of interest, Dale's middle name can be seen on the registration card to be Caruth.

The draft registration cards for your uncles[20] are shown on page 38 to 40, and your father's is reproduced on page 38. Several things can be discerned from the copy: He was 20 years old at the time, and was working on the farm of "S. G. Hartman" in Shabbona Grove, whom he also listed as next-of-kin. I can't make out the height and weight listed, but according to the card, your father had gray eyes and brown hair. If a better copy of his draft registration card would be of interest, it may be possible to obtain a better copy from the National Archives branch in Chicago, which is where I believe the originals for Illinois are kept.

Ray Ellis Hartman

I didn't take any steps to determine if your father actually was drafted or ever served in World War I, but if anyone in your family recalls hearing that he did serve, his records can most likely be obtained (for a fee, of course) from the friendly folks at the Military Personnel Center in St. Louis, Missouri.

All of Grier and Cynthia's children, including your father Ray, were still living at home in Paw Paw when the 1920 Census was taken (see page 41). By the time of the 1930 Census (see page 42), only Dale remained at home.

Grier died in Waterman, DeKalb County, Illinois on 28 January 1938. His wife Cynthia, who was living alone at the time of the 1940 census,[21] died on 19 October 1952 in Earlville, LaSalle County. The couple is buried in Wyoming Cemetery, Paw Paw, Lee County, IL.

---

[19] On the reproductions of these cards, the date appears to be 12 September 1915 rather than 12 September 1918, but the 1918 date is correct. For one thing, the draft hadn't been established in 1915; for another, the 12 September date for registration was established by law.

[20] ... other than Wilfred, who was only about 11 at the time, and too young to be accepted.

Your Dad appears with his parents in each of the censuses from 1900 through 1920. Throughout 1926 and 1927, the DeKalb Daily Chronicle Newspaper had various articles mentioning afternoon visits to the S. G. Hartman residence of a young lady identified as Miss Frances Griffin of Shabbona Grove, although these short entries make no mention of the purpose of these visits.

In the Monday, 20 February 1928 edition, however, the following blurb appeared:

> Mrs. Stearl Hartman and Duane, and Mrs. S.G. Hartman and Evelyn attended a miscellaneous shower at the Willis Lattin home near Shabbona Grove Saturday, in honor of Miss Frances Griffin who will soon become the bride of Roy (sic) Hartman.

– mystery solved. Despite much searching through Illinois civil and religious records (and even the DeKalb Daily Chronicle), I was unable to locate any actual record of their marriage (even using the name "Roy," but it seems safe to assume that it took place in the fall of 1928.

In July of 1929, their first daughter Genevieve (her mother Frances' middle name) was born.

The 1930 census shows your parents and your oldest sister Genevieve living in Shalbona Township, and is pictured on page 43. The most recent publicly available census, taken in 1940, shows you for the first time in Clinton Township, and is provided on page 45.

Your parents are, of course, buried in St. James Cemetery, Illinois.

"Miss Frances Griffin of Shabbona Grove"

---

[21] See page 44.

Suggestions for Further Research

To fill in more details about your Hartman ancestors, the following might prove useful:

LOCATION OF THE PALATINATE

♦ Continue the search for other Hartman households that may have arrived in Philadelphia from the Palatinate during the early to mid-eighteenth century to further expand the list of those who might be your original American ancestors.[22]

♦ A search for early nineteenth-century church meeting records for the Northumberland/Columbia/Montour County area to determine the Hartman's religious affiliation is probably not worth the effort. Knowing someone's religious affiliation can be useful when attempting to determine their country of origin, the timing of their immigration, and their reasons for coming to America, but even as late as John Hartman's pension application of 1833, he was unable to locate a clergyman as a witness because, as the application states, "there is no clergyman in the neighborhood." It therefore seems unlikely that there would have been a congregation that was sufficiently organized to maintain such records.

♦ Continue searching for 1830 census records for the Columbia County, Pennsylvania area; this may help determine when George and his family left his father's household, and when Phillip retired.

---

[22] One source that is accessible for free on the Internet is the web site: http://www.olivetreegenealogy.com/ships/palship_list.shtml

HARTMAN BRANCH ANCESTRY

Index of Illustrations: Hartman Family   Page

Ahnentafel Chart for Margaret Hartman Koester	17
Hartman Ancestry Diagram 1 of 4 for Margaret Hartman Koester	18
Hartman Ancestry Diagram 2 of 4 for Margaret Hartman Koester	19
Hartman Ancestry Diagram 3 of 4 for Margaret Hartman Koester	20
Hartman Ancestry Diagram 4 of 4 for Margaret Hartman Koester (with Caruth)	21
1790 Census: John Hartman Household in Hereford Twp, Berks Cty, Pennsylvania; National Archives Series m637, Roll 8, page 89	22
1790-1840 Census Transcriptions: Phillip and George Hartman Households	23
1790 Census: Phillip Hartman Household in Cocalico Twp, Lancaster Cty, Pennsylvania; National Archives Series m637, Roll 8, page 175 [info only – I doubt this is your family]	24
1800 Census: Phillip Hartman Household in Greenwood Twp, Northumberland Cty, Pennsylvania; National Archives Series m032, Roll 37, page 763	25
1810 Census: Phl Hartman Household in Mahoning Twp, Northumberland Cty, Pennsylvania; National Archives Series m252, Roll 53, page 164	26
1820 Census: Phillip Hartman Household in Mahoning Twp, Columbia Cty Pennsylvania; National Archives Series m033, Roll 101, page 41	27
1840 Census: Phillip and George Hartman Households in Hemlock Twp, Columbia Cty, Pennsylvania; National Archives Series m704, Roll 449, page 226	28
1850 Census: George Hartman Household in Hemlock Twp, Columbia Cty, Pennsylvania; National Archives Series m432, Roll 769, page 347	29
1850 Census: William Cox Household in Hemlock Twp, Columbia Cty, Pennsylvania; with Samuel Hartman; National Archives Series m432, Roll 769, page 345	30
1860 Census: George & Samuel Hartman Households in Hemlock Twp, Columbia Cty, Pennsylvania; National Archives Series m653, Roll 1098, page 811	31
1870 Census: Amos Hartman Household (with George) in Hemlock Twp, Columbia Cty, Pennsylvania; National Archives Series m593, Roll 1329, page 238b	32
1870 Census: Samuel & Samuel Hartman Households in West Hemlock Twp, Montour Cty, Pennsylvania; National Archives Series m593, Roll 1380, page 206	33
1880 Census: Samuel & Samuel G. Hartman Household ins West Hemlock Twp, Montour Cty, Pennsylvania; National Archives Series t9, Roll 1160, page 97	34
1900 Census: James Bredbender (?) Household in Center Township, Columbia County, Pennsylvania; National Archives Series t623, Roll 1398, page 189. (Samuel's son-in-law)	35
1900 Census: Grier Hartman Household in Paw Paw Township, DeKalb County, Illinois; National Archives Series t623, Roll 319, page 300b	36
1910 Census: Grier Hartman Household in Paw Paw Township, DeKalb County, Illinois; National Archives Series t624, Roll 284, page 220	37

Index of Illustrations: Hartman Family

	Page
12 September 1918 U.S. Draft Registration for Ray Hartman	38
5 June 1917 U.S. Draft Registration for Stearl J. Hartman	38
12 September 1918 U.S. Draft Registration for Dale Caruth Hartman	39
5 June 1917 U.S. Draft Registration for Arthur C. Hartman	39
5 June 1917 U.S. Draft Registration for Russell Hartman	40
1920 Census: Grier Hartman Household in Paw Paw Township, DeKalb County, Illinois; National Archives Series t625, Roll 303, page 138	41
1930 Census: Grier Hartman Household in Paw Paw Township, DeKalb County, Illinois; National Archives Series t626, Roll 510, page 4a	42
1930 Census: Ray Hartman Household in Shalbona Township, DeKalb County, Illinois; National Archives Series t626, Roll 510, page 6b	43
1940 Census: Cynthia Hartman in Earlville, LaSalle County; IL; National Archives Series t627, Roll 832, page 11b	44
1940 Census: Ray Hartman Household in Clinton Twp, DeKalb County, IL; National Archives Series t627, Roll 793, Page 001b	45

Ray Ellis and Frances Genevieve (Griffin) Hartman

Hartman Branch Ancestry

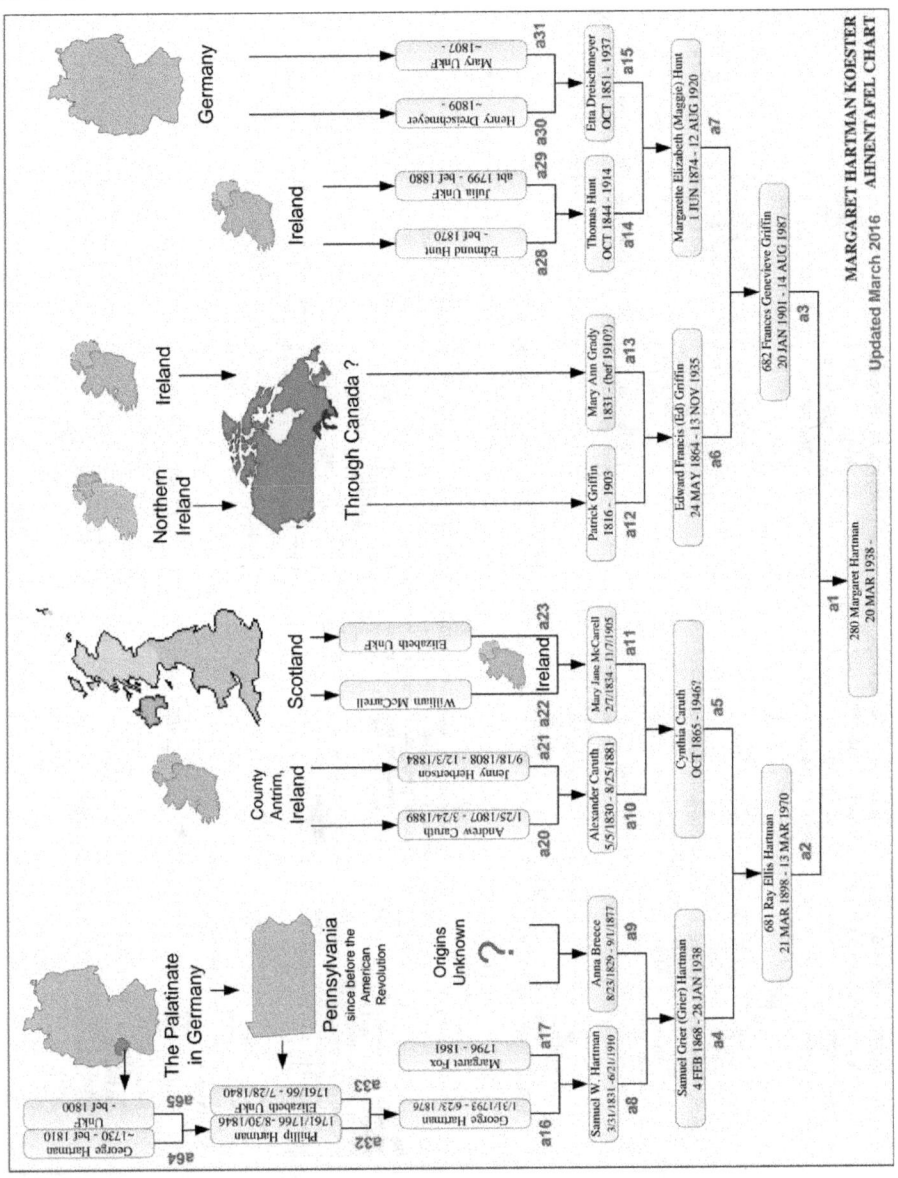

Ahnentafel Chart for Margaret Hartman Koester

HARTMAN – KOESTER ANCESTRY

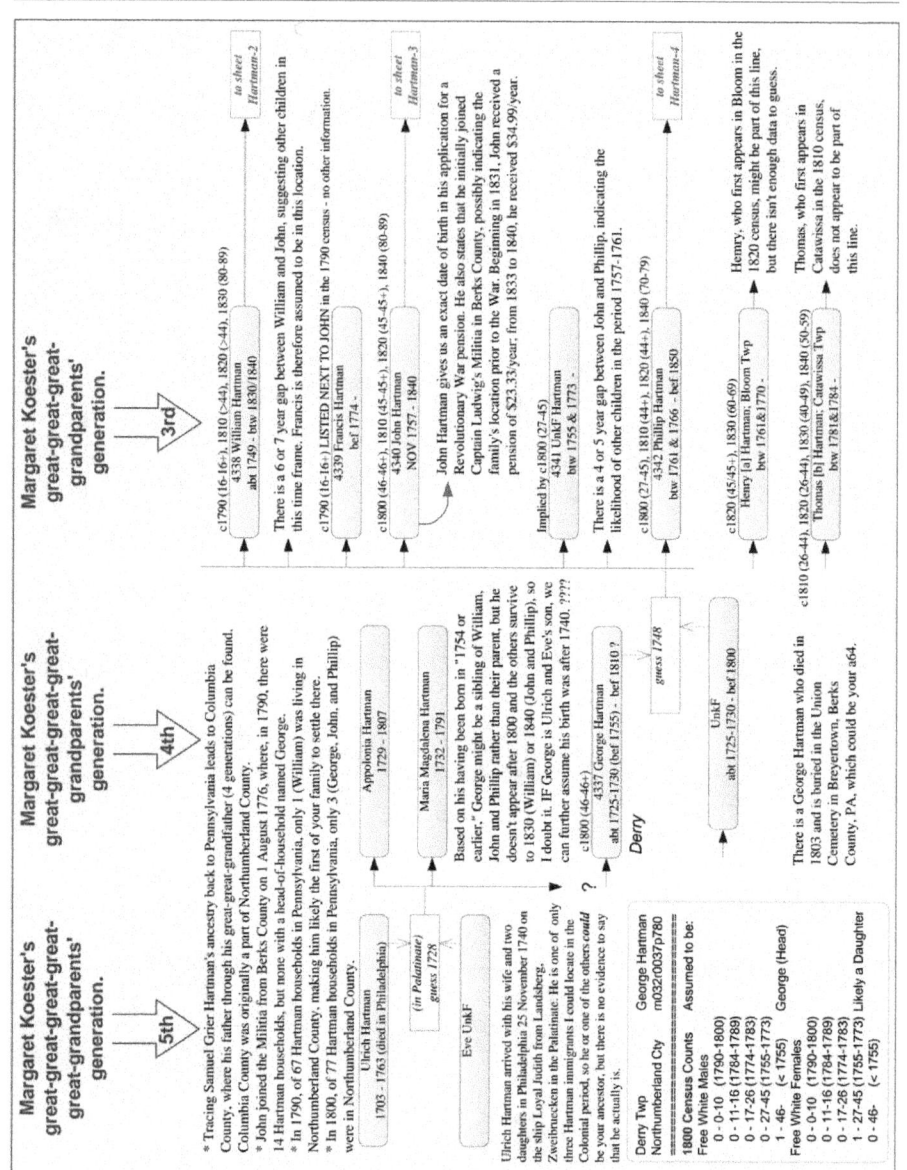

Hartman Ancestry Diagram 1 of 4 for Margaret Hartman Koester
The "to Hartman-4" reference from Philip Hartman points to the diagram on page 19.

Hartman Branch Ancestry

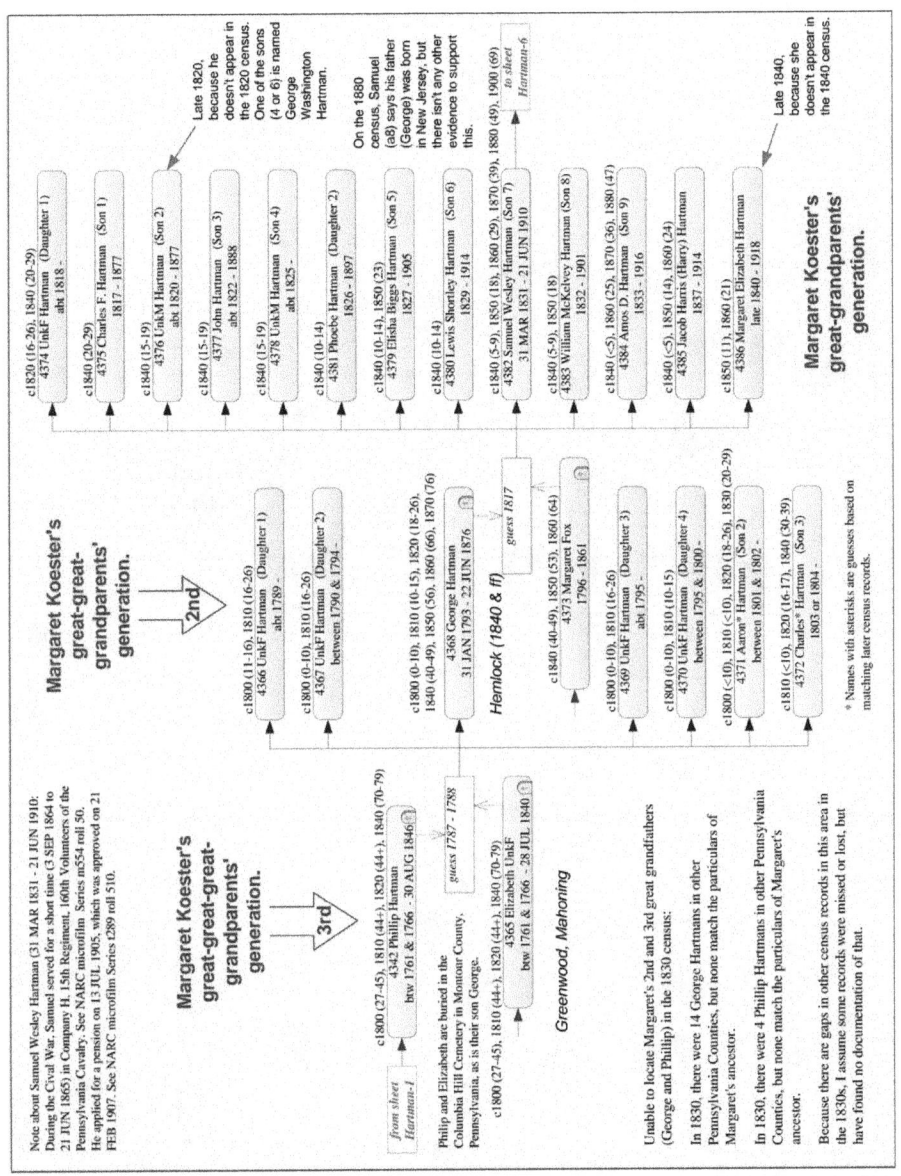

Hartman Ancestry Diagram 2 of 4 for Margaret Hartman Koester
The "from Hartman-1" reference pointing to Phillip Hartman comes from page 18
The "to Hartman-6" reference from Samuel W. Hartman points to the diagram on page 20.

Hartman – Koester Ancestry

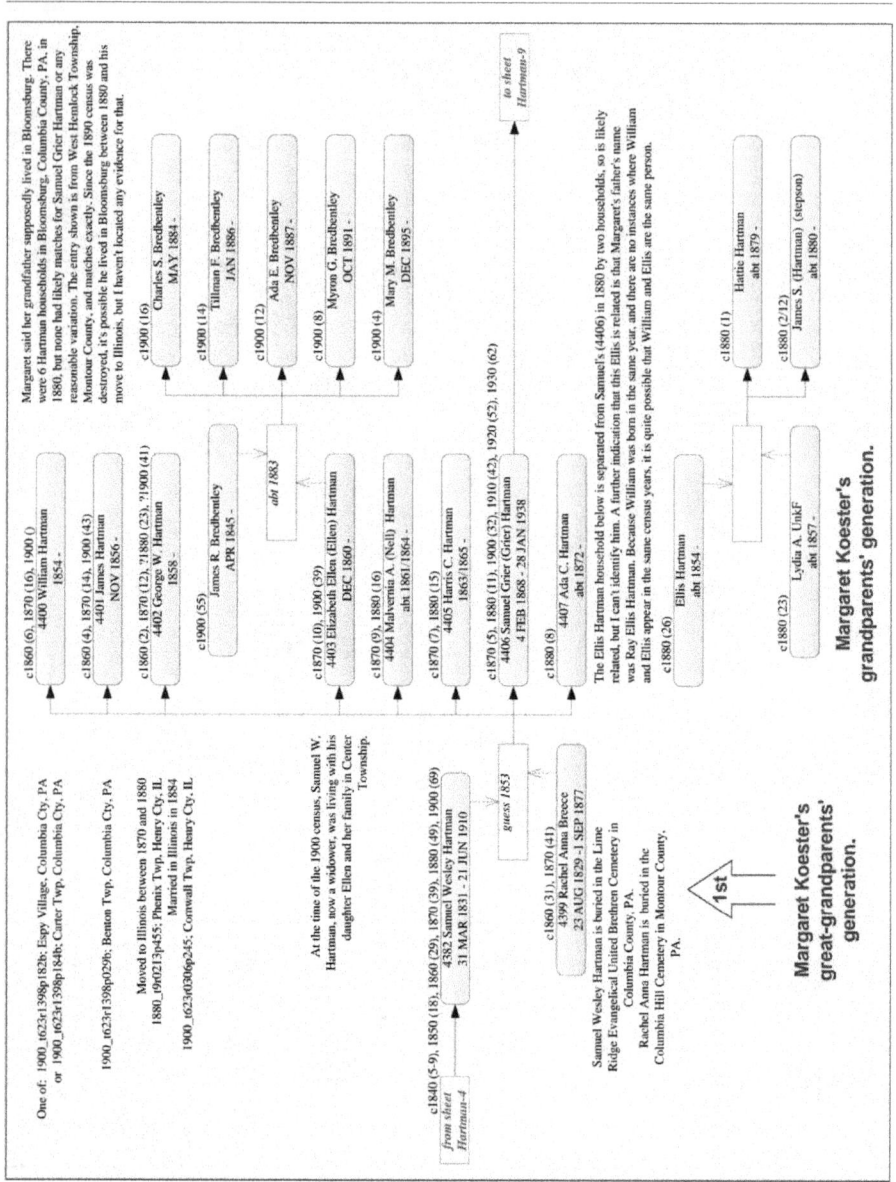

Hartman Ancestry Diagram 3 of 4 for Margaret Hartman Koester
The "from Hartman-4" reference pointing to Samuel W. Hartman comes from page 19
The "to Hartman-9" reference from Samuel G. Hartman points to the diagram on page 21.

HARTMAN BRANCH ANCESTRY

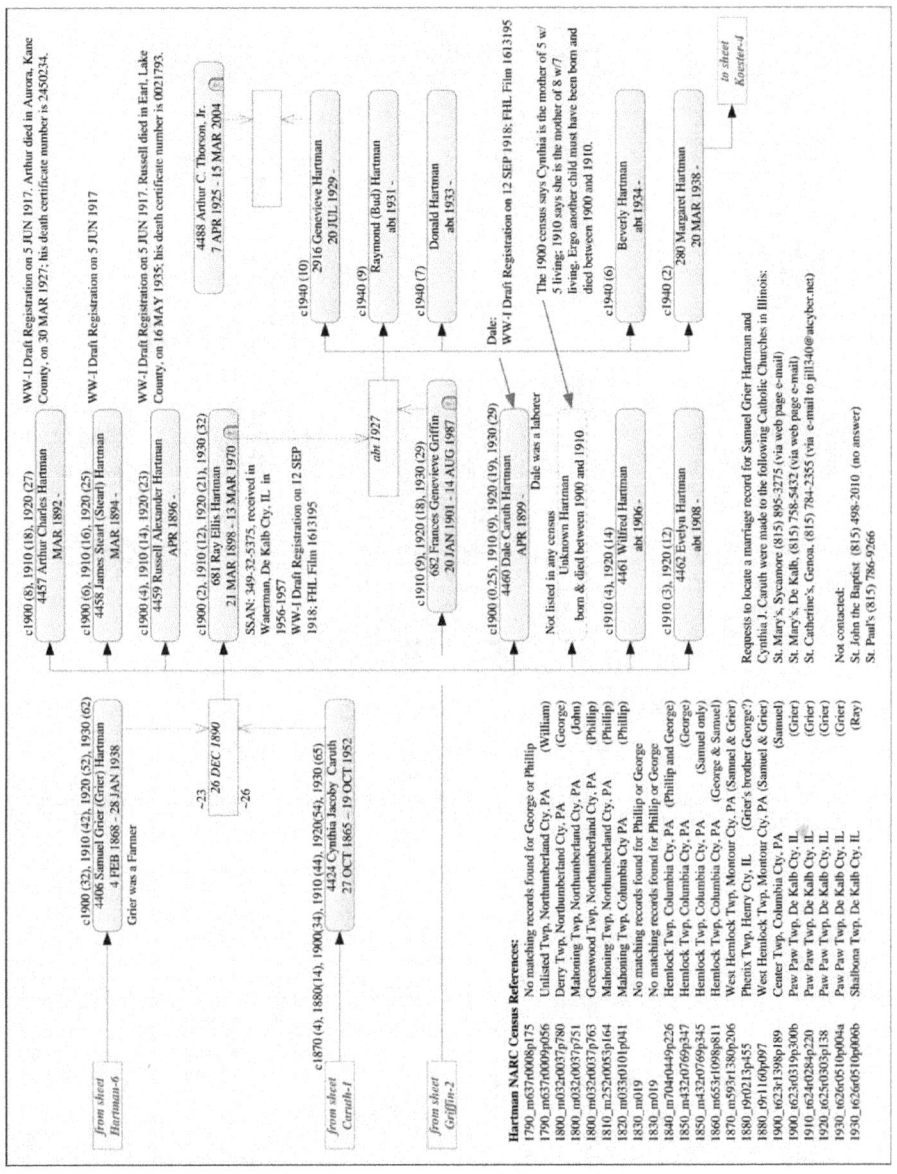

Hartman Ancestry Diagram 4 of 4 for Margaret Hartman Koester (Hartman-Caruth)
The "from Hartman-6" reference pointing to Samuel G. Hartman comes from page 20.
The "from Caruth-1" reference pointing to Cynthia J. Caruth comes from page 54.

1790 Census: John Hartman Household in Hereford Twp, Berks Cty, Pa
National Archives Series m637, Roll 8, page 89

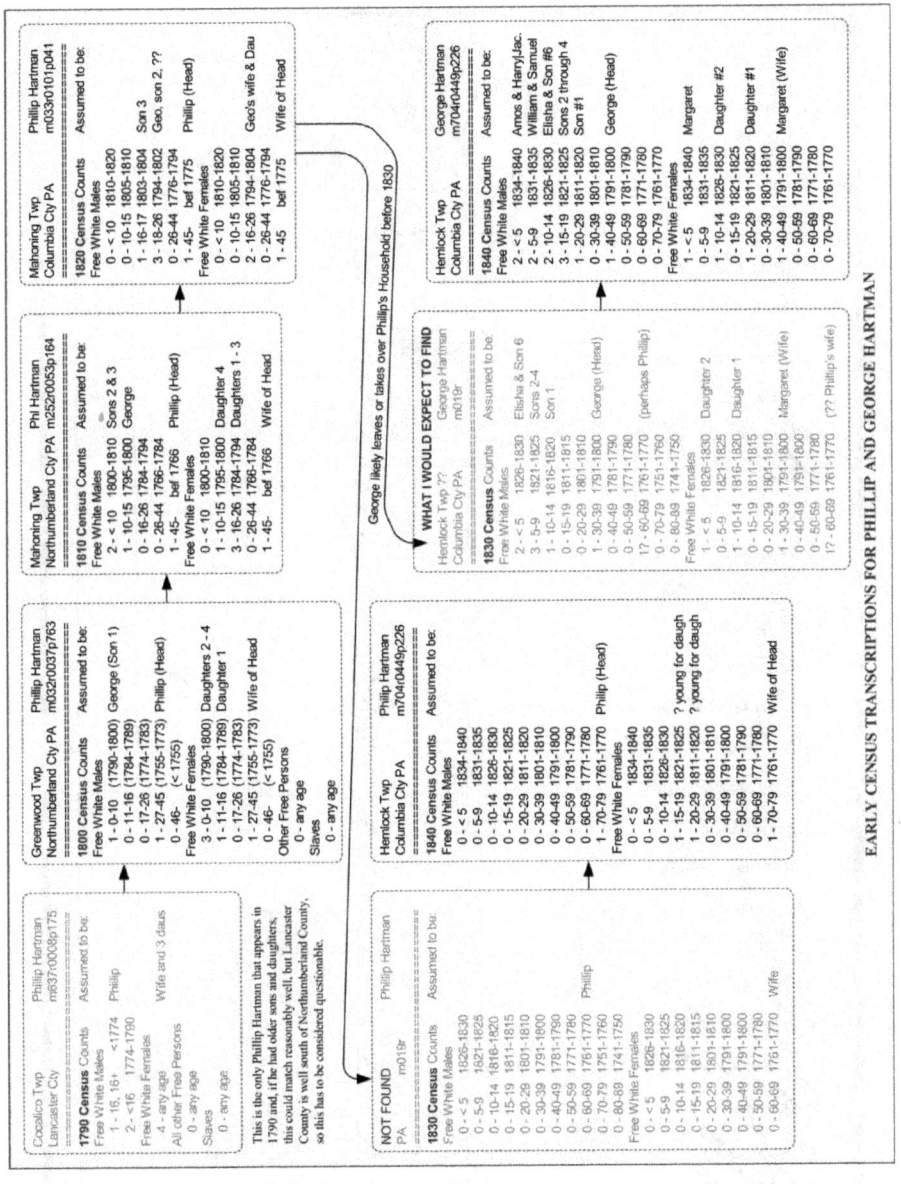

1790-1840 Census Transcriptions: Phillip and George Hartman Households

Since the early U.S. Census sheets are difficult to follow, this chart places all of the data for the relevant forms in an easier-to-read form. It also suggests what the missing 1830 census forms should look like if they are eventually located.

Names of Heads of Families	Free White Males of 16 years and upwards including heads of families	Free White Males under 16 years	Free White Females including heads of families	All other free persons	Slaves
Brought forward:	6990	6480	12489	385	233
Richael Adam	2		7		
Christr. Lutz	2		1		
Aron Biggs				2	
John Sehr	1	1	2		
Henry Bodenstal	1	1	2		
Jacob Ream		2	3		
John Himrich	1	2	2		
John Snyder	1	1	2		
Henry Braidels	2	2	3		
George Sillig	1		1		
Peter Smith	1	2	4		
James Bear	1	1	2		
Gabriel Laush	2	1	2		
Charles Trush	1	2	3		
Widow Troy		1	2		
Adam Trush	1	1	3		
John Singer	2	2	4		
Widow Alberds	1		3		
Henry Sole	1		1		
Jacob Hebliner	1		3		
George Heft	1	1	3		
Leonard Getz	3	2	5		
John Huber	1	2	3		
Jacob Huber	1	1	1		
Phillip Hartman	1	2	4		
John Eichdobe	2	2	4		
	7022	6510	12559	387	233

1790 Census: Phillip Hartman Household in Cocalico Twp, Lancaster Cty, Pa
National Archives Series m637, Roll 8, page 175 [info only]

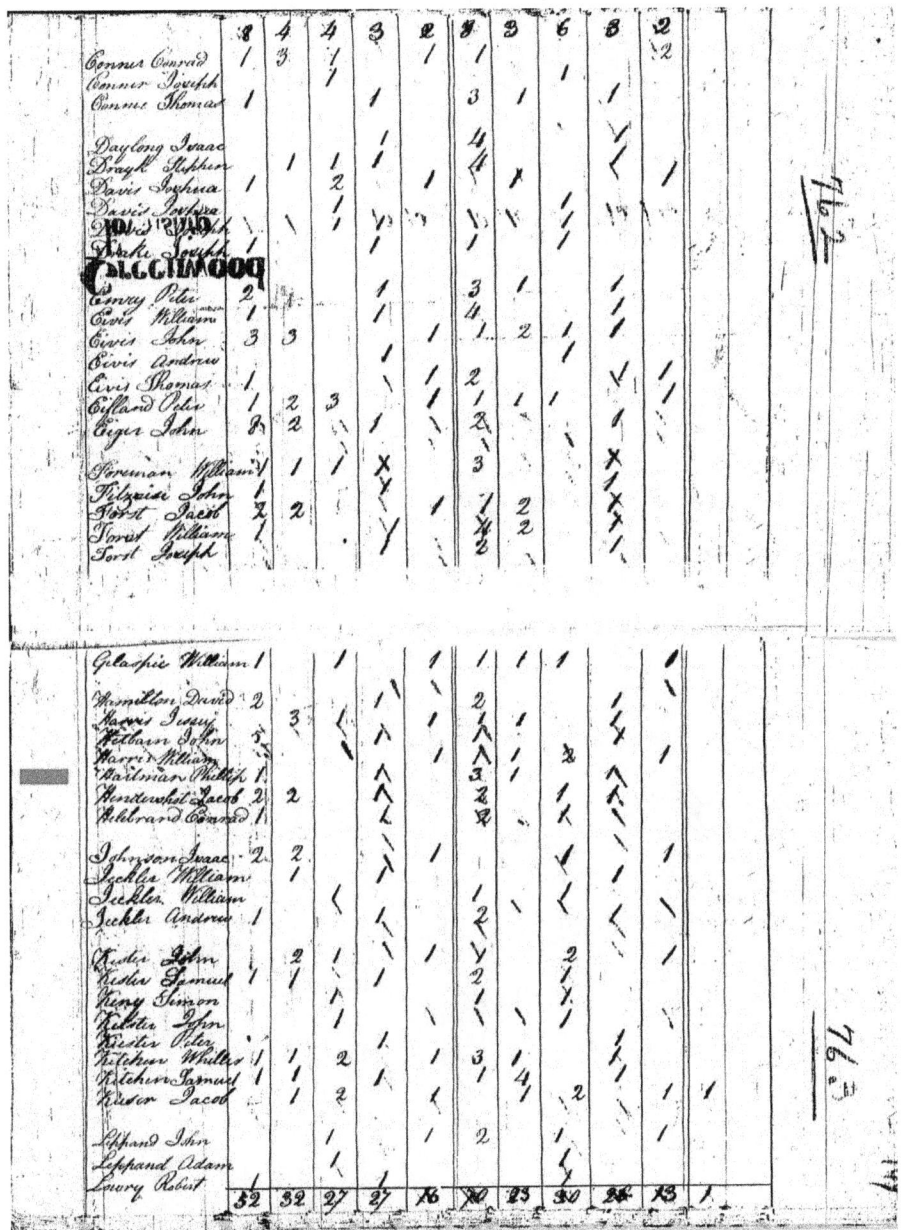

*1800 Census: Phillip Hartman Household: Greenwood Twp, Northumberland Cty, Pa
National Archives Series m032, Roll 37, page 763*

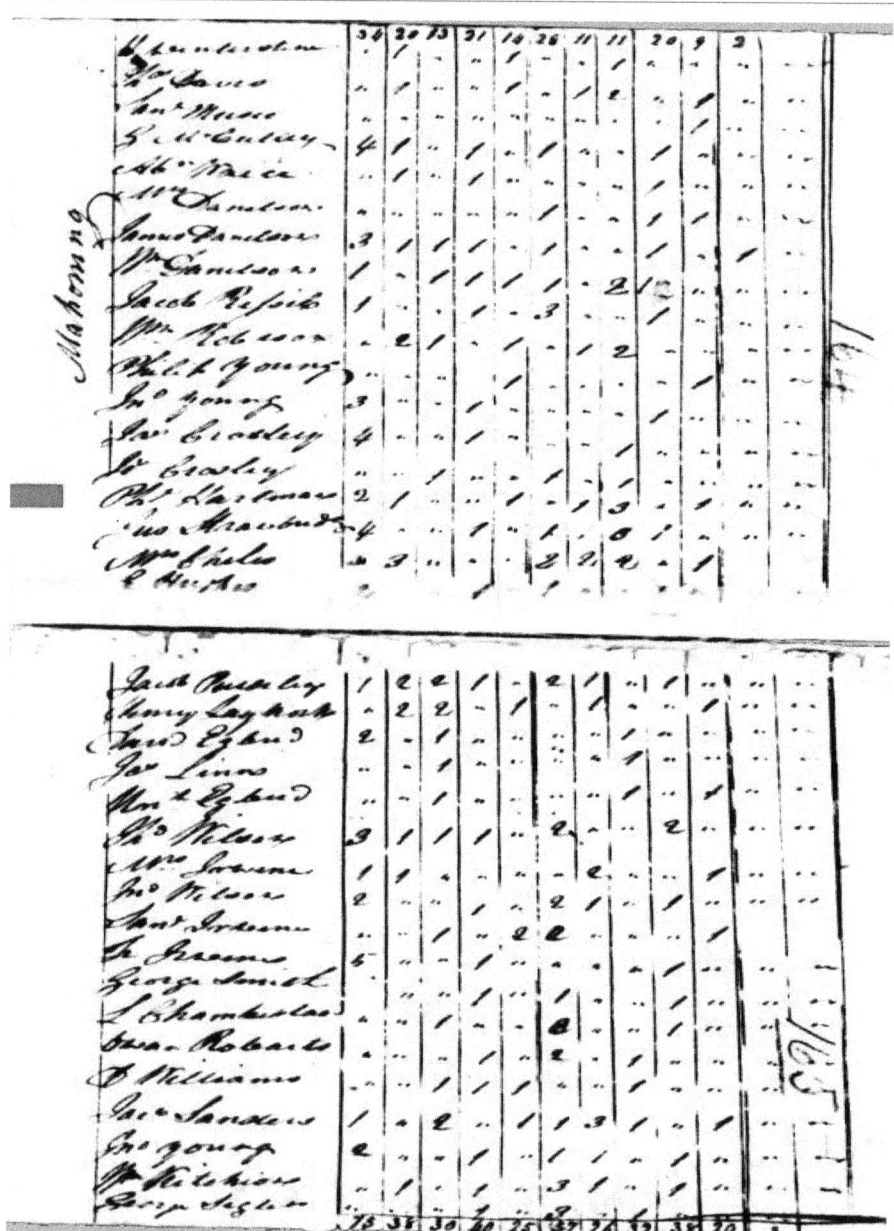

*1810 Census: Phl Hartman Household in Mahoning Twp, Northumberland Cty, Pa
National Archives Series m252, Roll 53, page 164*

1820 Census: Phillip Hartman Household in Mahoning Twp, Columbia Cty Pa
National Archives Series m033, Roll 101, page 41

1840 Census: Phillip & George Hartman Households in Hemlock Twp, Columbia Cty, Pa
National Archives Series m704, Roll 449, page 226

1850 Census: George Hartman Household in Hemlock Twp, Columbia Cty, Pa
National Archives Series m432, Roll 769, page 347

	Name	Age	Sex	Occupation	Value	Place of Birth				
	James P. Purcell	22	m	Laborer		Pa				1
	Elisha Purcell	21	m	Clerk		"				2
	Mary Purcell	19	f			"		1		3
	Martha Purcell	17	f			"		1		4
	Thomas? Purcell	13	m			"				5
	Dorothea Purcell	3	f			"				6
	Sarah J. Purcell	3	f			"				7
150	Peter Folmer	45	m	Laborer	400	"				8
	Eliz' Folmer	42	f			"				9
	Wm Folmer	15	m	Laborer		"				10
	Eliz' Folmer	13	f			"		1		11
151	Lee Cox	31	m	Carpenter	500	"				12
	Sarah Cox	22	f			"				13
	Sarah A. Cox	7	f			"		1		14
152	Wm Gillespie	33	m	Carpenter	400	"				15
	Harriet Gillespie	29	f			"				16
	John Gillespie	7	m			"		1		17
	Ruth Gillespie	6	m			"		1		18
	David Gillespie	5	m			"				19
	Sarah Gillespie	3	f			"				20
	Almira Gillespie	½	f			"				21
153	Sidney I. Slater	40	m	Farmer	300	NJ				22
	Mary Slater	50	f			Pa				23
	Henry Slater	20	m	Laborer		"				24
	Rachael Walton	15	m	do		"		1		25
	Cornelia A. Worthington	19	f			"				26
154	Wm Cox	32	m	Farmer		"				27
	Thirza E. Cox	32	f			"				28
	Levi A. Cox	5	m			"				29
	Mm L Cox	3	m			"				30
	E. A Cox	1	m			"				31
	Eliz' Robbins	35	f			"				32
	Saml Hartman	18	m	Laborer		"				33
155	Emaline Evans	56	f			"				34
	Robt Evans	19	m	Laborer		"				35
	Anne Evans	15	f			"		1		36
	Jeremiah Evans	12	m			"		1		37
156	Jacob Purcell	35	m	Farmer		"				38
	Mary Purcell	34	f			"				39
	Wellington Purcell	13	m			"		1		40
	Thos H. Purcell	6	m			"		1		41
	James Purcell	3	m			"				42

1850 Census: William Cox Hhd in Hemlock Twp, Columbia Cty, Pa; w/Samuel Hartman
National Archives Series m432, Roll 769, page 345

1860 Census: George & Samuel Hartman Households in Hemlock Twp, Columbia Cty, Pa
National Archives Series m653, Roll 1098, page 811

*1870 Census: Amos Hartman Household (w/George) in Hemlock Twp, Columbia Cty, Pa
National Archives Series m593, Roll 1329, page 238b*

1870 Census: Samuel Hartman Households in West Hemlock Twp, Montour Cty, Pa
National Archives Series m593, Roll 1380, page 206

Hartman – Koester Ancestry

1880 Census: Samuel Hartman Household in West Hemlock Twp, Montour Cty, Pa
National Archives Series t9, Roll 1160, page 97

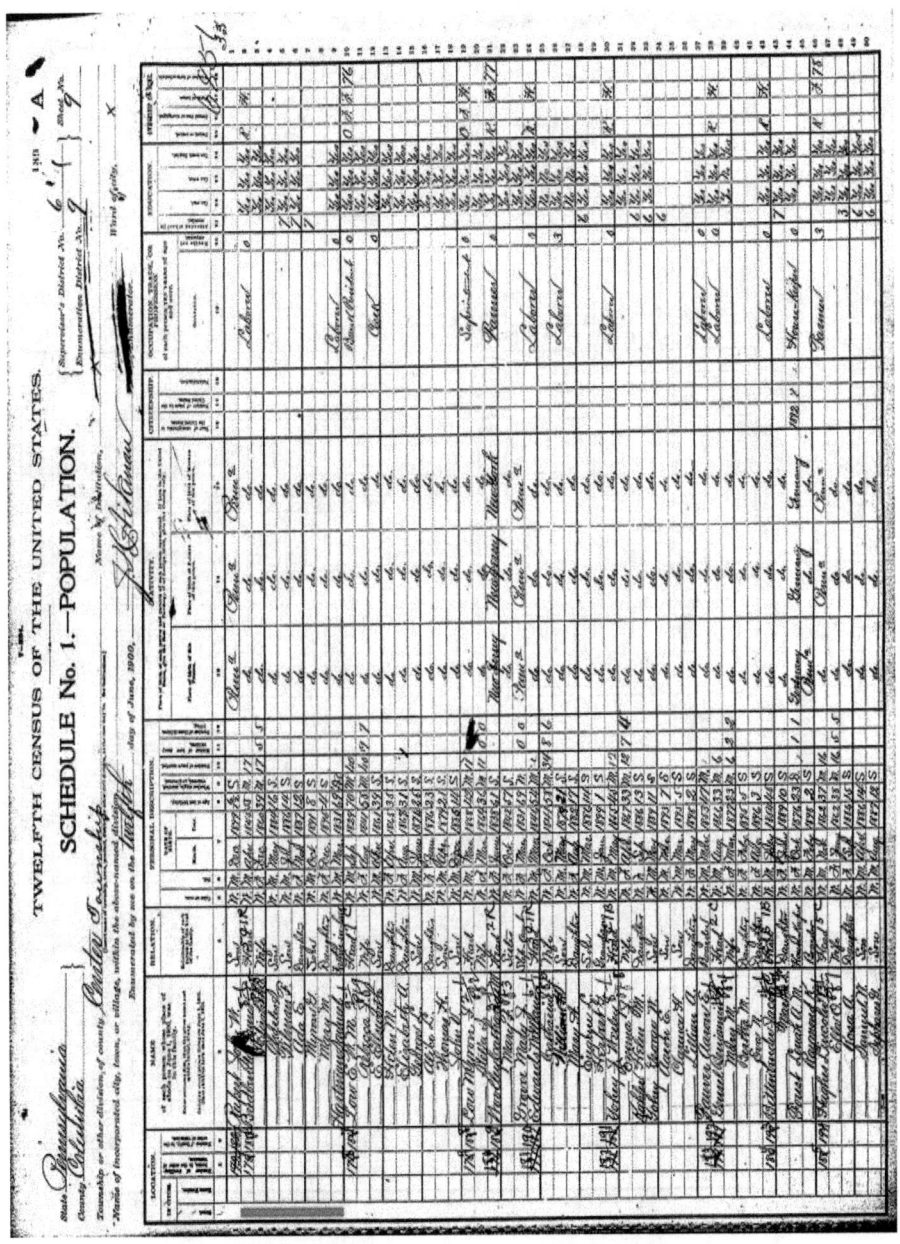

1900 Census: James Bredbender (?) Household in Center Twp, Columbia County, Pa National Archives Series t623, Roll 1398, page 189. (Samuel Hartman's son-in-law)

*1900 Census: Grier Hartman Household in Paw Paw Twp, DeKalb County, IL
National Archives Series t623, Roll 319, page 300b*

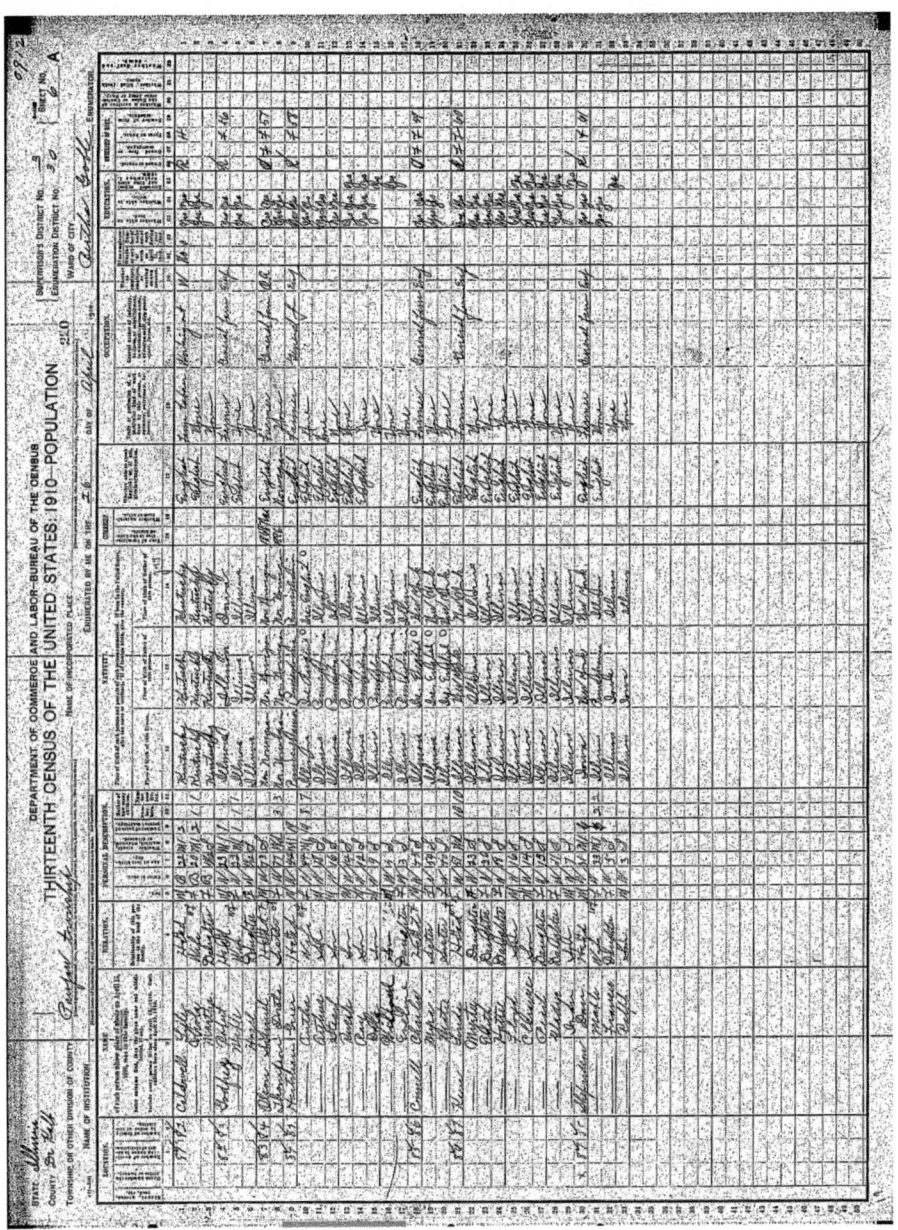

*1910 Census: Grier Hartman Household in Paw Paw Twp, DeKalb County, IL
National Archives Series t624, Roll 284, page 220*

12 September 1918 U.S. Draft Registration Card for Ray Ellis Hartman

5 June 1917 U.S. Draft Registration Card for Stearl J. Hartman

Hartman Branch Ancestry

12 September 1918 U.S. Draft Registration Card for Dale Caruth Hartman

5 June 1917 U.S. Draft Registration Card for Arthur C. Hartman

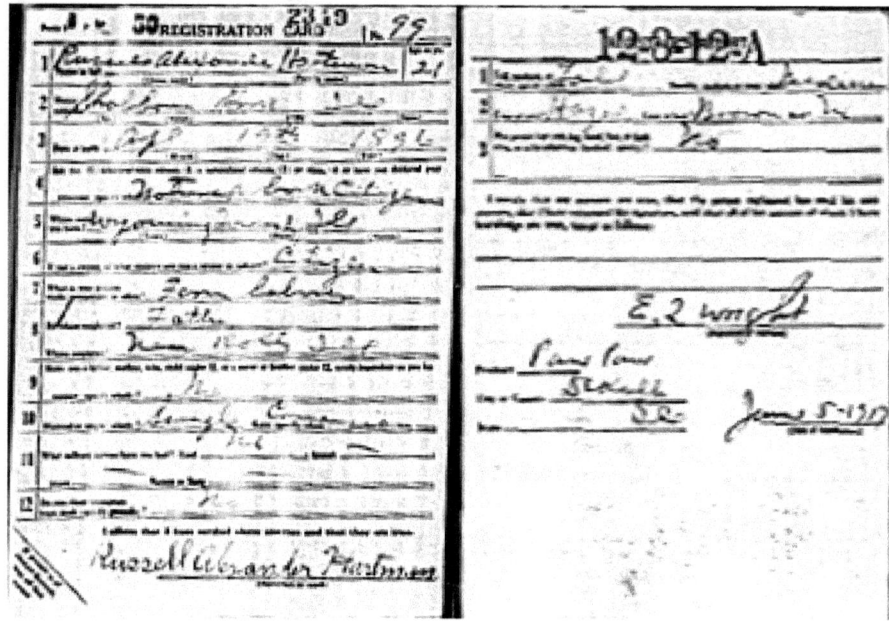

5 June 1917 U.S. Draft Registration Card for Russell Hartman

1920 Census: Grier Hartman Household in Paw Paw Twp, DeKalb County, IL
National Archives Series t625, Roll 303, page 138

Hartman – Koester Ancestry

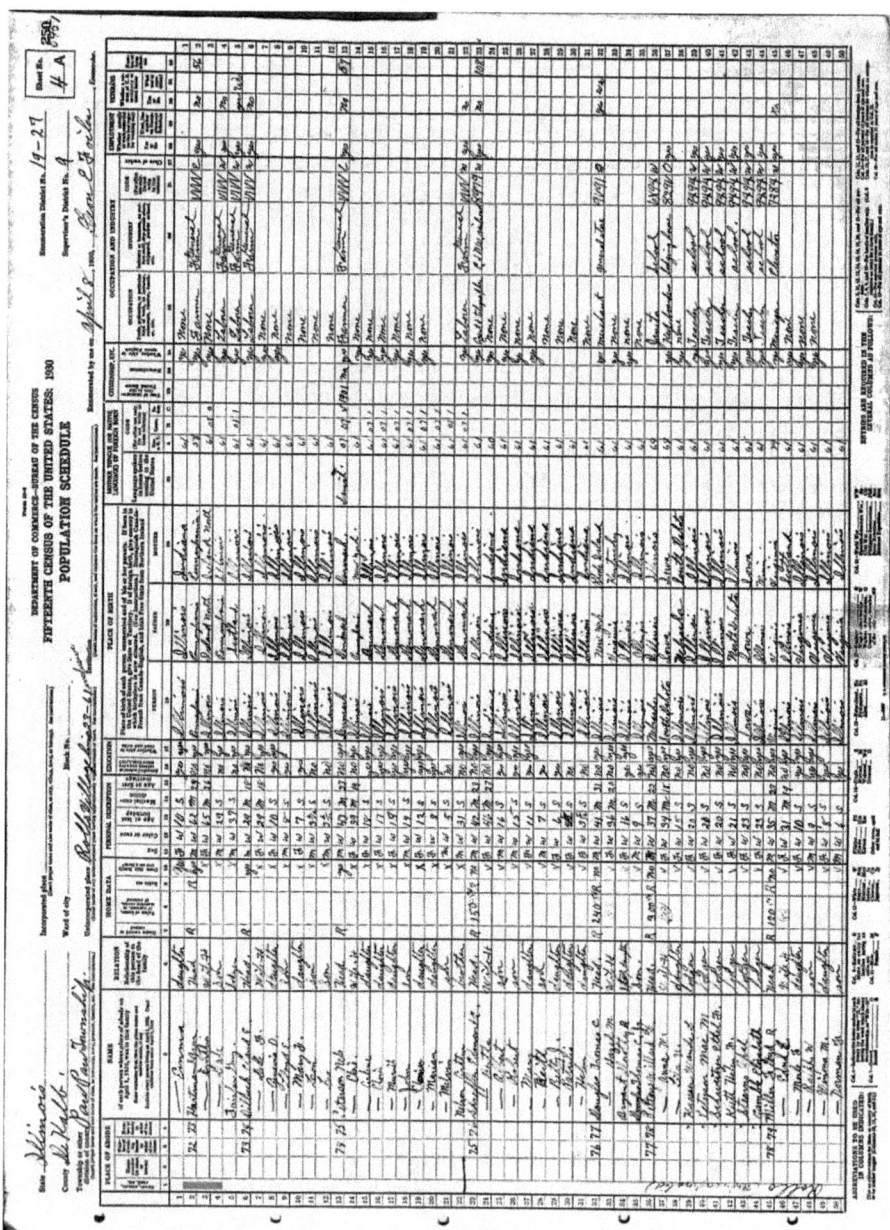

1930 Census: Grier Hartman Household in Paw Paw Twp, DeKalb County, IL
National Archives Series t626, Roll 510, page 4a

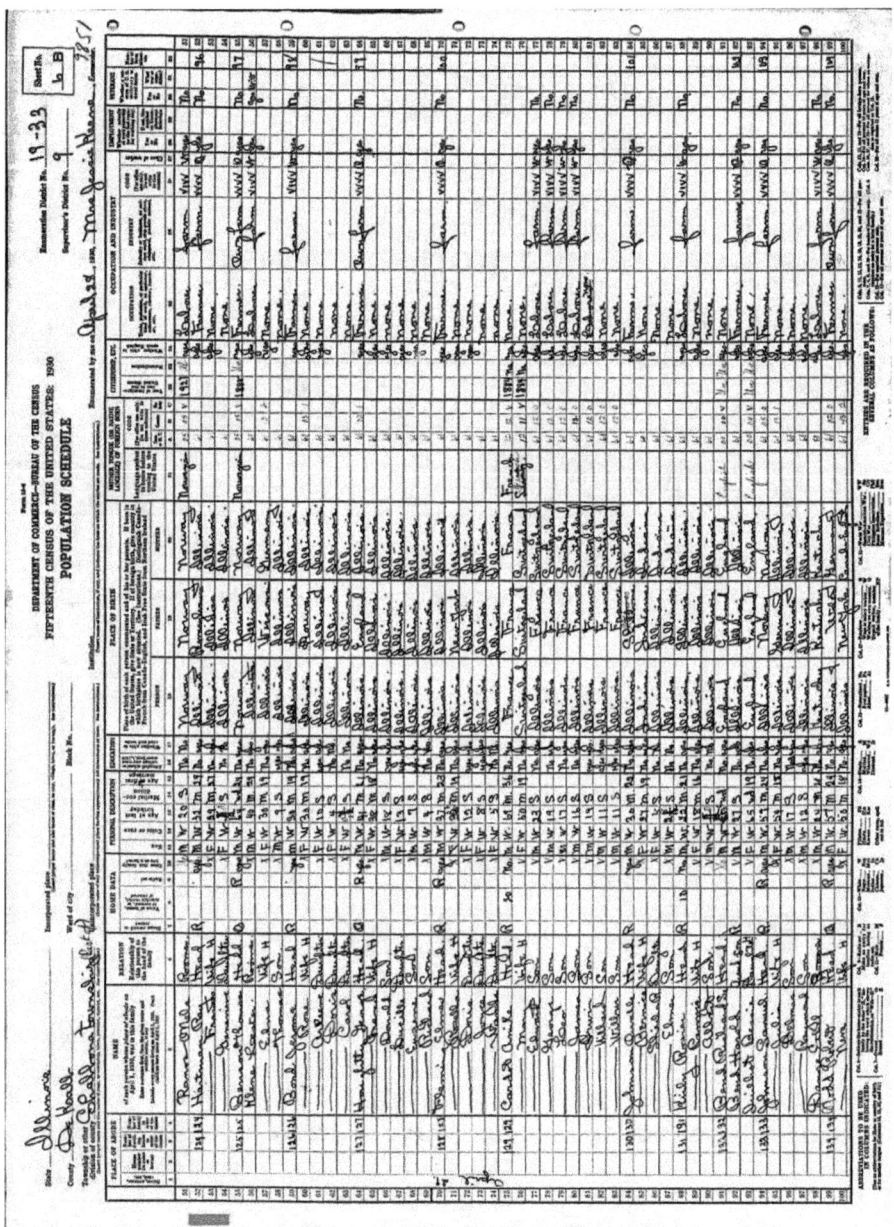

*1930 Census: Ray Hartman Household in Shalbona Twp, DeKalb County, IL
National Archives Series t626, Roll 510, page 6b*

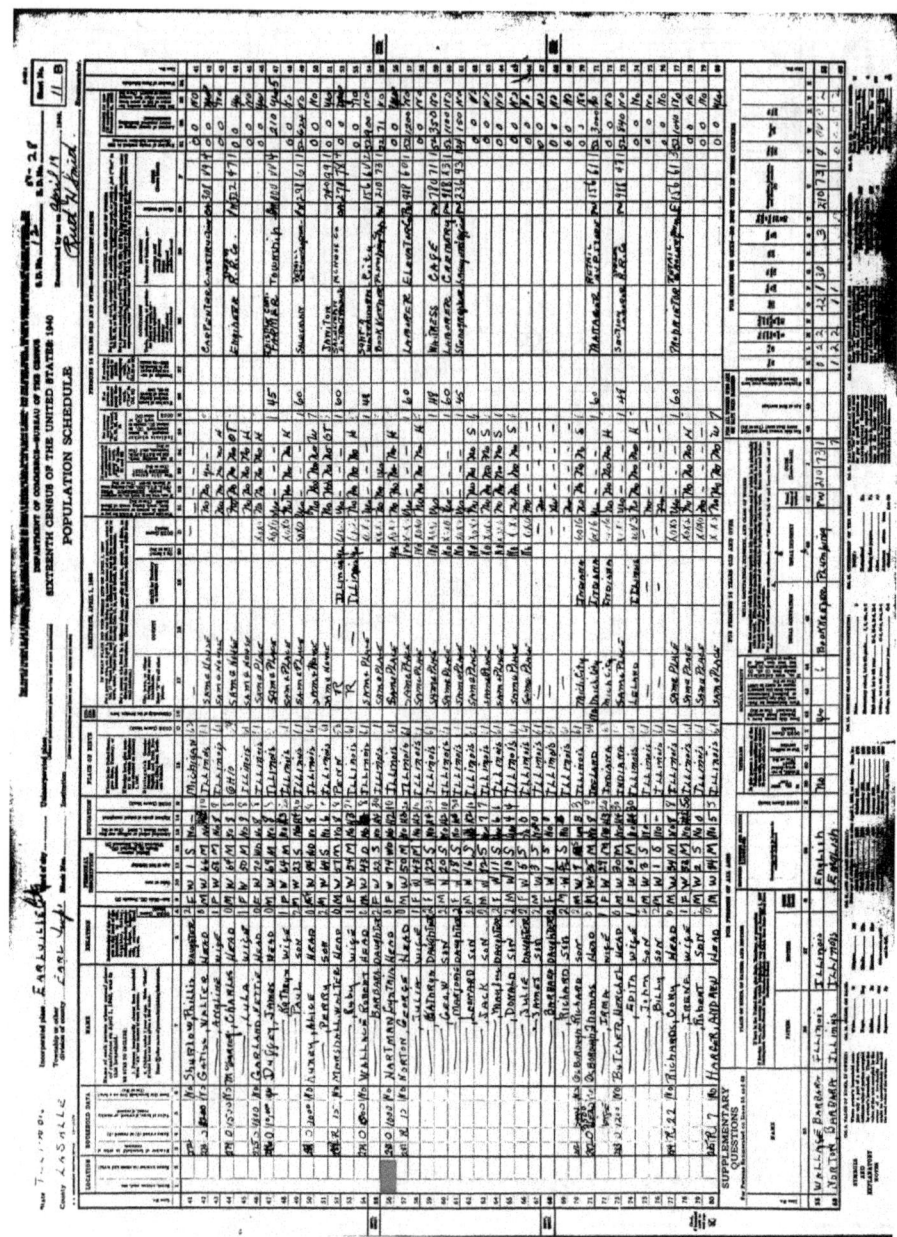

1940 Census: Cynthia Hartman in Earlville, LaSalle County; IL
National Archives Series t627, Roll 832, Page 11b

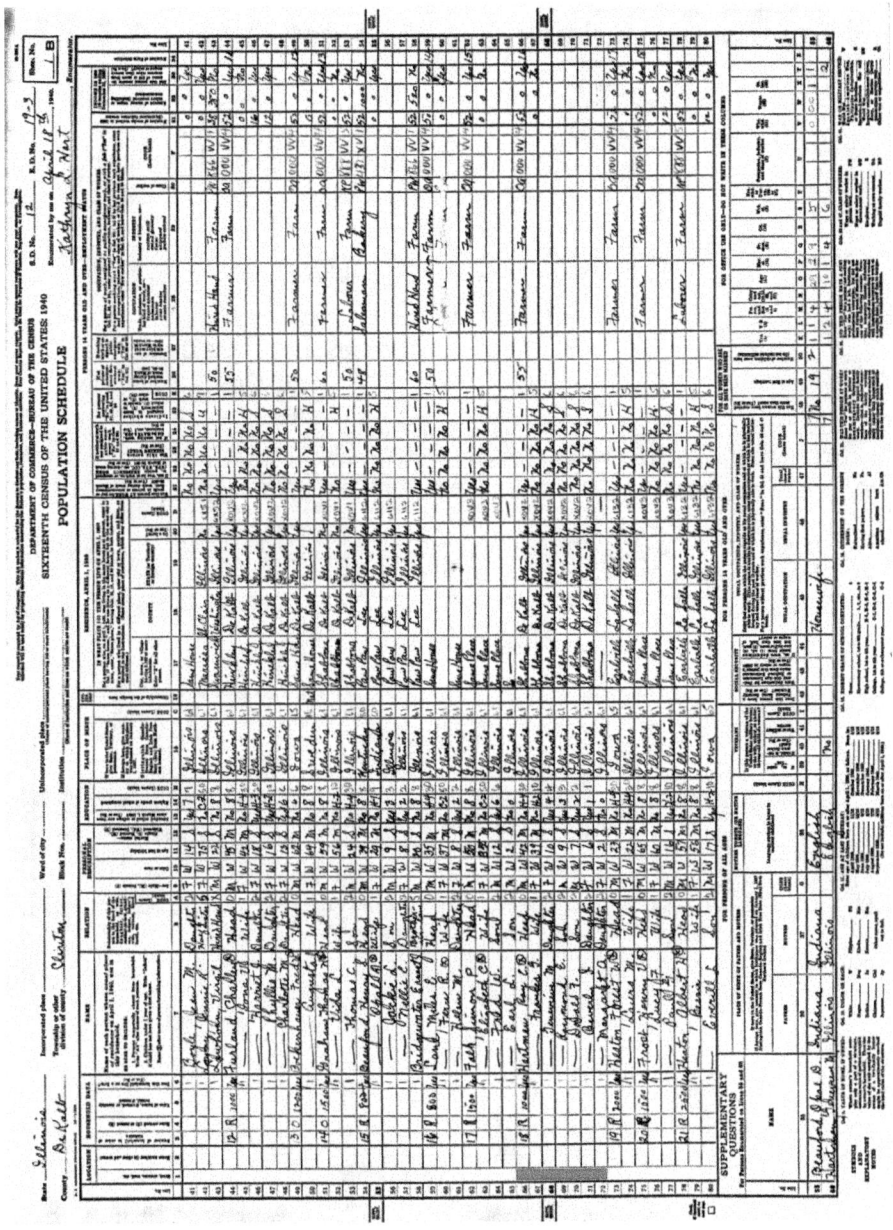

1940 Census: Ray Hartman Household in Clinton Twp, DeKalb County, IL
National Archives Series t627, Roll 793, Page 001b

My Grandsons' Hartman-side Ahnentafel Chart

An Ahnentafel chart showing my Grandsons' Koester-side is on page 131.

Caruth Ancestry

Your paternal grandmother Cynthia Jacoby Caruth was born in Illinois on 27 October 1865, and married your grandfather Samuel Grier Hartman, who was

> MY GRANDMOTHER
> CYNTHIA (CARUTH) HARTMAN
> PAW PAW, IL.
> BORN - DON'T KNOW
> DIED - DON'T KNOW (MAYBE 1946)
> I don't know anything about Cynthia's parents.

approximately three years younger than she was, the day after Christmas in 1890; Cynthia would have been about twenty-six years old then. Copies of the 1900 and subsequent census forms on which she appears are included in the earlier "Hartman Ancestry" section on pages 36, 37, 41, and 42.

Cynthia's grandfather (your 2nd great-grandfather) Andrew Caruth was born in County Antrim in Northern Ireland on 25 January 1807. By the early 1820s, the potato famine and mass starvation had begun taking hold in Ireland, leading to decades of poverty and civil unrest. Nonetheless, in approximately 1828 or 1829, your great-great-grandfather Andrew married Jane Herbertson (known as Jennie), who was also born in County Antrim on 18 September 1808, and they began a family – a rather optimistic undertaking in the Ireland of that era.

Andrew Caruth (1807-1889)

Jennie Herbertson Caruth (1808-1884)

In 1835, Gustave de Beaumont, a well-traveled French sociologist, visited Ireland and recorded his perspective of the Ireland of the time:

> "I have seen the Indian in his forests, and the Negro in his chains, and thought, as I contemplated their pitiable condition, that I saw the very extreme of human wretchedness; but I did not then know the condition of unfortunate Ireland ... In all countries, more or less, paupers may be discovered; but an entire nation of paupers is what was never seen until it was shown in Ireland."

County Antrim is one of six counties that formed what is today called Northern Ireland, although the Irish themselves often refer to it as Ulster – despite the fact that Ulster itself originally included another three counties.

Children of Andrew and Jennie Herbertson Caruth

Andrew and Jennie, pictured above in contemporary charcoal drawings, had at least eight children in Antrim that I could find, including two pairs of twins. The first of their children was your direct ancestor Alexander, who was born on 5 May 1830. Their last children, the twins James and William, were born in 1848. See the ancestry diagram on page 54 for more details of the Caruth family. The four-to-five-year gap between Alexander and his next oldest identified siblings suggests that there may have been other children who didn't survive; a similar gap exists between the fourth and fifth sons (Matthew and Robert).

In early 1851, presumably after the birth of his twins James and William, Andrew left his family in Ireland to establish himself in the United States. He arrived in Boston on the ship Clara Wheeler on 9 July 1851. A Caruth descendant now living in Virginia[23] told me the family tradition is that he went to stay with his wife Jennie's brother in Washington County, Pennsylvania. Although the name Herbertson is recorded on Jennie's tombstone, there seems to be some doubt as to whether it might actually be Halverson, Harbison, or some other variant. In any case, I was unable to locate anyone with any similar surname in Washington County that seemed to be a reasonable match in the 1850 census.[24]

So far, in fact, I have been unable to locate any firm evidence of Andrew's presence in the United States until about twenty years later.

In 1853, most likely in late spring, Andrew's wife Jennie crossed over to Liverpool, England[25] with her eight children, and from there boarded the ship Enter-

---

[23] Who, by the way, is the source of the images of your Caruth ancestors in this section.

[24] It seemed reasonable to me that if Andrew left to join him in 1851 or thereabouts, Jennie's brother would likely have already been living there by the time of the 1850 census.

[25] This part is a guess. It is also possible that the entire family had gone to Liverpool, England in 1850 or so with Andrew, and remained there without him until they eventually departed for New York, but temporary living with eight children seems unlikely.

prise for passage to New York. The oldest child, Alexander, pictured below, was by this time twenty-one years old, and the others ranged from the fifteen-year-old twins Andrew and Jane to the youngest twins who were only two.

Although traveling with eight children has undoubtedly always been stressful, it was certainly more so in the mid-nineteenth century because of the living environment on the ships. The Caruths wisely avoided what were known as the "coffin ships" sailing directly from Ireland to the United States in that period, but conditions in general were appalling enough that the United States Congress passed a law in 1848 to establish standards for any ships that transported passengers to or from this country. A one-page summary of this bill, shown on page 55, was required to be distributed to the captains of each ship that arrived in any U.S. port over the next few years. A quick reading of these new "minimum standards," along with the implicit assumption that these were intended to be improvements over existing conditions, will provide some insight into what travel must have been like, and – by extension – how strong the passengers' motivations must have been to undertake that travel.

Alexander Caruth (May 1830 – Aug 1881)

Jennie and her children arrived in New York on the twelfth of September in 1853 to rejoin Andrew, presumably at her brother's residence.

Portions of the passenger manifest for the Enterprise are shown on pages 56 (the header page, showing details of the ship) and 57 (the second page of the manifest, showing the Caruth family). Like many Irish passenger manifests of this time, there seems to be no separation of classes indicated on the list (e.g. "cabin" and "steerage" would be typical). This suggests that the Enterprise was not originally designed with passenger transport in mind, and was therefore one of many pressed into service by the maritime shipping companies to take advantage of the large numbers of emigrants during this period.

Note on the manifest that, immediately above Jane and her children, there is another "Alexander Caruth" shown who is the same age as her son (your ancestor Alexander was listed as "Alex, age 20"), followed by a "Grace McBurney, age 21." Their proximity in the list suggests that they were traveling together with your ancestors' family, and therefore probably related in some way, but whatever relationship there might be isn't obvious.

The Caruth family is known to have lived in Pennsylvania, Virginia[26] and Ohio before settling in Cottage Hill, Illinois in 1862. I haven't yet been able to locate the family in the 1860 census, although if they were traveling during the time the census was being taken, that might explain their absence.

By 1870, only three of their children were still living at home with them, now in Wyoming Township in Lee County, Illinois; see page 58 and 59). In 1880, Andrew and Jennie, then both seventy-one years old, were living alone in Wyoming Township (see page 61).

Jennie died on 3 December 1884; her husband Andrew died on 24 March 1889. Although Andrew moved to Hamilton County, Iowa[27] after Jennie's death, he is buried with Jennie in Cottage Hill Cemetery[28] in Paw Paw, Lee County, Illinois.

The McCarrells

Your 2nd great-grandparents William M. and Elizabeth McCarrell lived in Ballymena Parish in County Antrim, Ireland, and had at least four children between about 1829 and 1834[29], the last of whom was your great-grandmother Mary Jane, born on 7 March 1834. On the 1870 census (see page 60), Mary Jane indicated that her parents had both been born in Scotland.

After Mary Jane's birth, her father William, then 37, and his 40 year old brother Patrick left for America on the S.S. Garonne, arriving in New York on 20 January 1836.

It was four and a half years before Eliza (as Elizabeth was known) was able to bring the couple's four daughters aboard the S.S. Trenton on 14 July 1840 for the journey to New York. The family arrived there on the 27th of July, and joined William, who seems to have settled in the area west of Pittsburgh.

Mary Jane eventually married Andrew and Jennie Caruth's oldest known son Alexander on 17 February 1857 in Brooke County, Virginia – also west of Pittsburgh, which would become the northern panhandle of West Virginia as the Civil War began.

---

[26] ... although the parts where they lived became part of West Virginia at the onset of the Civil War, when that section of the state decided to remain with the Union.
[27] See the map on page 89. Hamilton County is six across and four down from the top.
[28] Sometimes known as Presbyterian Cemetery.
[29] The first three were Eliza, b. abt 1829, Rose, b. abt 1831, and Bridget, b. abt 1833.

Children of Alexander and Mary Jane McCarrell Caruth

In the first of several moves, the couple settled in Belmont County, Ohio in 1858, and by 1864, Alexander and Mary Jane Caruth had had their first four children – all daughters. As with his father Andrew's family, details of Alexander's family can also be seen in the ancestry diagram on page 54.

When the Confederate forces attacked Fort Sumter on April 12, 1861, precipitating the Civil War, three of the Caruth brothers would have been old enough to have possibly participated. Alexander was about 30 – certainly not at the high end of military service for that era – and Matthew and Robert were 21 and 16 respectively.

I have been able to locate no records suggesting that Alexander served during the Civil War and, in any case, he continued to have children throughout the war,[30] so I think it is safe to say that he was never in the military. I was also unable to find any mention of Matthew in any Civil War rosters, but there is a Robert J. Caruth who served in the Union Army with the 126th Illinois Infantry. Since I believe your Caruth ancestors were still in Ohio at this time, I suspect this is not Andrew's son, but a different Robert Caruth[31] who will be mentioned below.

Alexander and Mary Jane McCarrell Caruth

After the war, in November 1866, both Alexander's family and that of his parents Andrew and Jennie Caruth moved to Lee County in Illinois, settling in Paw Paw and Brooklyn Townships respectively. I've found nothing to suggest why the Caruth family may have relocated to Illinois, but it should be noted that remnants of another Caruth family (a mother and four children ranging from twenty-five to eighteen years old) were living in Illinois at the time of the 1860 census. This could easily be dismissed as coincidence, except that two of the children, Robert and Alex, were twins, making a relationship somewhat more likely. This, by the way, is the Robert that I suspect served in the Civil War.

---

[30] The couple's four daughters were born during the period from 1860 to 1865.
[31] Alexander's brother Robert married Rebecca Coss in Ohio 1867, tending to support this.

Once settled in Brooklyn Township, Mary Jane had the couple's fifth, sixth, and seventh children, including their only son, Thomas, born in about 1868. Your grandmother Cynthia, born in October of 1865, was their fifth child, and the first to be born in Illinois.

By 1880, Alexander and Mary Jane had relocated to Wyoming Township (see page 62). Alexander died on the 25th of August the following year and, like his parents would later be, was buried (right) in Cottage Hill Cemetery. Mary Jane remained living with her son Thomas and his family at least until the time of the 1900 census (see page 63), although when she died on 7 November 1905, she was listed as living in Aurora, Illinois. Mary Jane was also buried in Cottage Hill Cemetery.

As an interesting anecdote regarding the 1880 census, Alexander and Mary Jane's fourth child Sarah A. Caruth, who was known as Sadie, was not only listed in the Caruth household, but was also listed in the household of David C. Hoag of Paw Paw Township, where she was working as a servant at the time.

Suggestions for Further Research

To fill in more details about your Caruth ancestors, the following might prove useful:

- Attempt to locate Andrew Caruth in the period from when he arrived in 1851 until his family arrived in 1853.

- Locate a marriage record for Alexander Caruth and Mary Jane McCarrell. I have been provided with another document suggesting they were actually married in Canonsburg Pennsylvania (rather than in Brooke County), but I have been unable to substantiate either one.

- Locate Andrew, Jane/Jennie, and/or Alexander Caruth in the 1860 census – likely in Ohio, but they may have been somewhere else between their arrival in the United States and the birth of their second daughter Mary M. Caruth, (also called Linie) who was born in Ohio in about 1860.

Index of Illustrations: Caruth Family · Page

Caruth Ancestry Diagram 1 of 1 for Margaret Hartman Koester	54
May 1848 – An early "Passenger Bill of Rights" giving an idea of shipboard conditions at the time the Caruths came to the United States	55
12 Sep 1853 Passenger Manifest of the Enterprise: Liverpool to New York; National Archives Series m237, Roll 131, List 950, page 1 (Caruth Family)	56
12 Sep 1853 Passenger Manifest of the Enterprise: Liverpool to New York; National Archives Series m237, Roll 131, List 950, page 2 (Caruth Family)	57
1870 Census: Andrew Caruth Household in Paw Paw Twp, Lee County, Illinois; National Archives Series m593, Roll 246, page 509a	58
1870 Census: Andrew Caruth Household in Paw Paw Twp, Lee County, Illinois; National Archives Series m593, Roll 246, page 509b	59
1870 Census: Alexander Caruth Household in Brooklyn Twp, Lee Cty, Illinois; National Archives Series m593, Roll 246, page 256	60
1880 Census: Andrew Caruth Household in Wyoming Township, Lee County, Illinois; National Archives Series t9, Roll 225, page 451	61
1880 Census: Alexander Caruth Household in Wyoming Township, Lee County, Illinois; National Archives Series t9, Roll 225, page 450	62
1900 Census: Thomas A. Caruth Household (with widowed mother Mary Jane Caruth) in Wyoming Township, Lee County, Illinois;	63

HARTMAN – KOESTER ANCESTRY

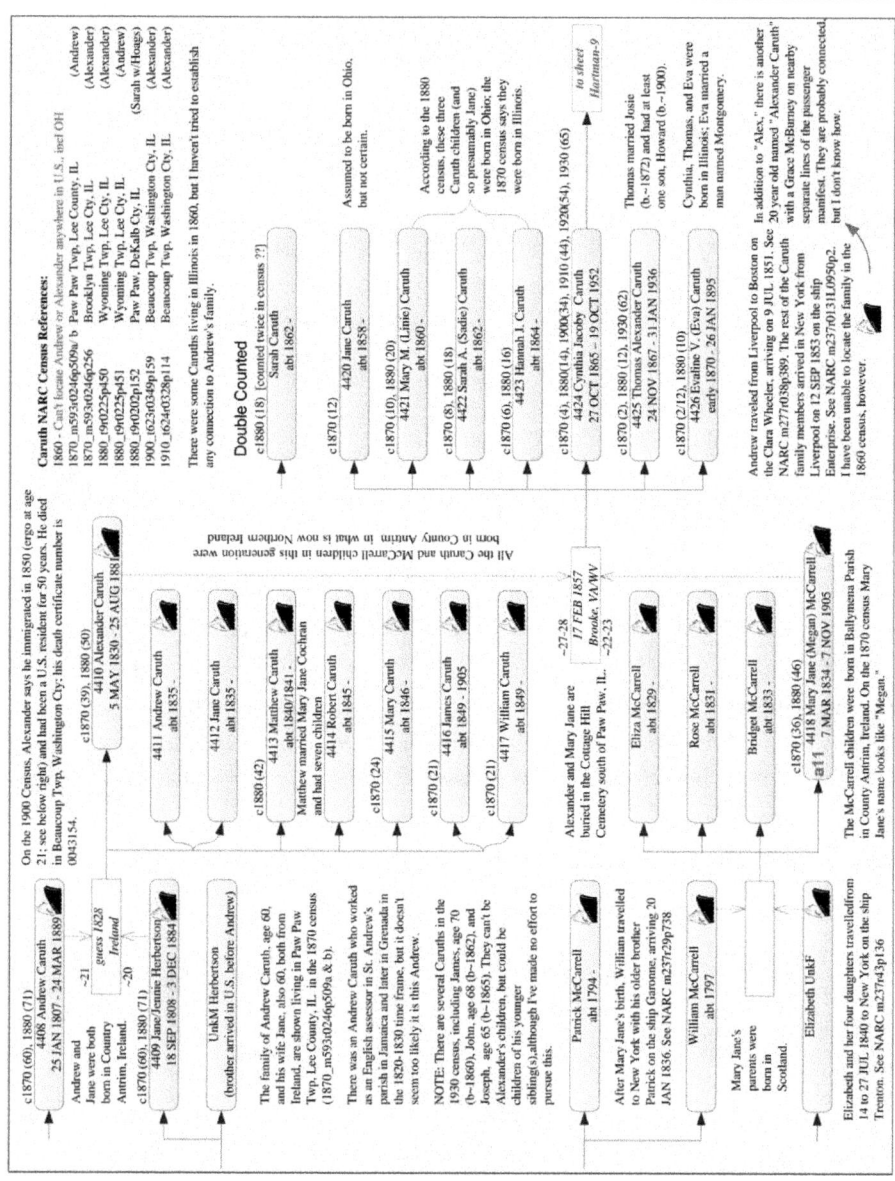

Caruth Ancestry Diagram 1 of 1 for Margaret Hartman Koester
The "to Hartman-9" reference from Cynthia Caruth points to the diagram on page 21.

AND YOU THINK YOU HAVE IT BAD - A notice to Ships' Captains about an Act of Congress passed in May 1848

[Handwritten: Collector]

AN ACT to provide for the Ventilation of Passenger Vessels, and for other purposes.

Be it enacted by the Senate and House of Representatives of the United States of America in Congress assembled, That all vessels, whether of the United States or any other country, having sufficient capacity, according to law, for fifty or more passengers, (other than cabin passengers,) shall, when employed in transporting such passengers between the United States and Europe, have on the upper deck, for the use of such passengers, a house over the passage way leading to the apartment allotted to such passengers below deck, firmly secured to the deck, or coamings of the hatch, with two doors, the sills of which shall be at least one foot above the deck, so constructed, that one door or window in vessels so employed, and having the capacity to carry two hundred and fifty such passengers or more, shall have two such houses, and the stairs, or ladder, leading down to the aforesaid apartment, shall be furnished with a hand-rail of wood or strong rope: *Provided,* nevertheless, booby hatches may be substituted for such houses in vessels having three permanent decks.

SEC. 2. *And be it further enacted,* That every such vessel so employed, and having the legal capacity for more than one hundred such passengers, shall have at least two ventilators, to purify the apartment or apartments occupied by such passengers; one of which shall be inserted in the after part of the apartment or apartments, and the other shall be placed in the forward portion of the apartment or apartments, and one of them shall have an exhausting cap to carry off the foul air, and the other a receiving cap to carry down the fresh air; which said ventilators shall have a capacity proportioned to the size of the apartment or apartments to be purified, namely, if the apartment or apartments will lawfully authorize the reception of two hundred such passengers, the capacity of such ventilators shall, each of them, be equal to a tube of twelve inches in diameter in the clear, and in proportion for larger or smaller apartments, and all said ventilators shall rise at least four feet and six inches above the upper deck house, and be of the most approved form and construction: *Provided,* That if it shall appear, to the satisfaction of the collector of the customs of the port from which the vessel is about to depart, that such vessel is equally well ventilated by any other means, such other means of ventilation shall be deemed, and held to be, a compliance with the provisions of this section.

SEC. 3. *And be it further enacted,* That every vessel carrying more than fifty such passengers, shall have for their use on deck, housed and conveniently arranged, at least one caboose or cooking range, the dimensions of which shall be equal to four feet long, and one foot six inches wide, for every two hundred passengers, and provision shall be made in the manner aforesaid in this ratio for a greater or less number of passengers: *Provided, however,* And nothing herein contained shall take away the right to make such arrangements for cooking, between decks if that shall be deemed desirable.

SEC. 4. *And be it further enacted,* That, all vessels employed as aforesaid, shall have on board, for the use of such passengers, at the time of leaving the best port whence such vessel shall sail, well secured under deck, for each passenger, at least fifteen pounds of good navy bread, ten pounds of rice, ten pounds of oat meal, ten pounds of wheat flour, ten pounds of peas and beans, thirty-five pounds of potatoes, one pint vinegar, sixty gallons fresh water ten pounds of salted pork, free of bone, all to be of good quality, and a sufficient supply of fuel for cooking; but at places where either rice, oat meal, wheat flour, or peas and beans cannot be procured, of good quality, and on reasonable terms, the quantity of either or any of the other last named articles may be increased and substituted therefor; and in case potatoes cannot be procured on reasonable terms, one pound of either of said articles may be substituted in lieu of five pounds of potatoes; and the captains of such vessels shall deliver to each passenger at least one-tenth part of the aforesaid provisions weekly, commencing on the day of sailing; and daily at least three quarts of water, and sufficient fuel for cooking; and if the passengers on board of any such vessel in which the provisions, water, or fuel, herein required, shall not have been provided as aforesaid shall, upon their arrival at the port to which they are bound, make complaint thereof, upon oath, before the collector of such port, the master or owner of any such vessel shall pay to each and every passenger, who shall have been put on short allowance, the sum of three dollars for each and every day they may have been on such short allowance, to be recovered in the circuit or district court of the United States: *Provided,* nevertheless, And nothing herein contained shall prevent any passenger, if the master of the vessel shall furnish him in good order, it shall fully satisfy the provisions of this act so far as regards food: And *provided further,* That any passenger may also, with the consent of the captain, furnish for himself a sufficient for the articles of food required in other and different articles; and if without waste or neglect on the part of the passenger, they shall prove insufficient, and the captain shall furnish, comfortable, from the ship's stores during the residue of the voyage, this in regard to food shall also be a compliance with the terms of this act.

SEC. 5. *And be it further enacted,* That the captain of any such vessel so employed is hereby authorized to maintain good discipline, and such habits of cleanliness among such passengers as will tend to the preservation and promotion of health; and to that end he shall cause such regulations as he may adopt for this purpose to be posted up, before sailing, on board such vessel, in a place accessible to such passengers, and shall keep the same so posted up, during the voyage; and it is hereby made the duty of said captain to cause the apartment occupied by such passengers to be kept, at all times, in a clean, healthy state; and the owners of every such vessel are hereby required to construct the decks, and all parts of said apartment, so that it can be thoroughly cleansed; and they shall also provide a safe, convenient privy or water closet, for the exclusive use of every hundred such passengers. And when the weather is such that said passengers cannot be mustered on deck with their bedding, it shall be the duty of the captain of every such vessel to cause the deck, occupied by said passengers, to be cleansed with chloride of lime, or some other equally efficient disinfecting agent, and also at such other times as said captain may deem necessary.

SEC. 6. *And be it further enacted,* That the master and owner or owners of any such vessel so employed, which shall not be provided with the house or houses over the passage ways, as prescribed in the first section of this act; or with the ventilators, as prescribed in the second section of this act; or with the cabooses or cooking ranges, with the houses over them, as prescribed in the third section of this act; shall severally forfeit and pay to the United States the sum of two hundred dollars for each and every violation of, or neglect to conform to, the provisions of said sections; and fifty dollars for each and every neglect or violation of any of the provisions of the fifth section of this act; to be recovered by suit in any circuit or district court of the United States, within the jurisdiction of which the said vessel may arrive, or from which it may be about to depart, or at any place within the jurisdiction of such courts, wherever the owner or owners, or captain of such vessel, may be found.

SEC. 7. *And be it further enacted,* That the collector of the customs, at any port in the United States at which any vessel so employed shall arrive, or from which any such vessel shall be about to depart, shall appoint and direct one of the inspectors of the customs for such port to examine such vessel, and to report in writing to such collector, whether the provisions of the first, second, and fifth sections of this act have been complied with in respect to such vessel, and if such, have been complied, compliance, and be approved by such collector, it shall be deemed and held as conclusive evidence thereof.

SEC. 8. *And be it further enacted,* That the first section of the act entitled "An Act to regulate the carriage of passengers in merchant vessels," approved February twenty-second, eighteen hundred and forty-seven, be so amended, that when the height of distance between the decks of the vessels referred to in said section, shall be less than six feet and not less than five feet there shall be allowed to each passenger sixteen clear superficial feet on the deck, instead of fourteen, as prescribed in said section; and if the height or distance allowed to each, passenger less than five feet, there shall be allowed to each passenger twenty-two clear superficial feet on the deck; and if the master of any such vessel shall take on board of such vessel, in any port of the United States, a greater number of passengers, in proportion to the space designated in said first section of the act of eighteen hundred and forty-seven, or if the master or any such vessel shall take on board, at a foreign port, and bring within the jurisdiction of the United States, a greater number of passengers than is allowed by this section, said master shall be deemed guilty of a misdemeanor, and upon conviction thereof shall be punished in the manner provided for the punishment of persons convicted of a violation of the act aforesaid; and in computing the number of passengers on board such vessels, all children under the age of one year, at the time of embarkation, shall be excluded from such computation.

SEC. 9. *And be it further enacted,* That this act shall take effect in respect to such vessels sailing from ports in the United States, in thirty days from the time of its passage, and in respect to every such vessel sailing from ports in Europe, in sixty days after such approval; and it is hereby made the duty of the Secretary of State, to give notice, in the ports of Europe, of this act, in such manner as he may deem proper.

SEC. 10. *And be it further enacted,* That so much of the first section of the act entitled "An Act regulating passenger ships and vessels," approved March second, eighteen hundred and nineteen, or any other act that limits the number of passengers to two for every five tons, is hereby repealed.

[APPROVED, MAY 17, 1848.]

May 1848 – An early "Passenger Bill of Rights" giving an idea of shipboard conditions at the time the Caruths came to the United States

*12 September 1853 Passenger Manifest of the Enterprise: Liverpool to New York
National Archives Series m237, Roll 131, List 950, page 1*

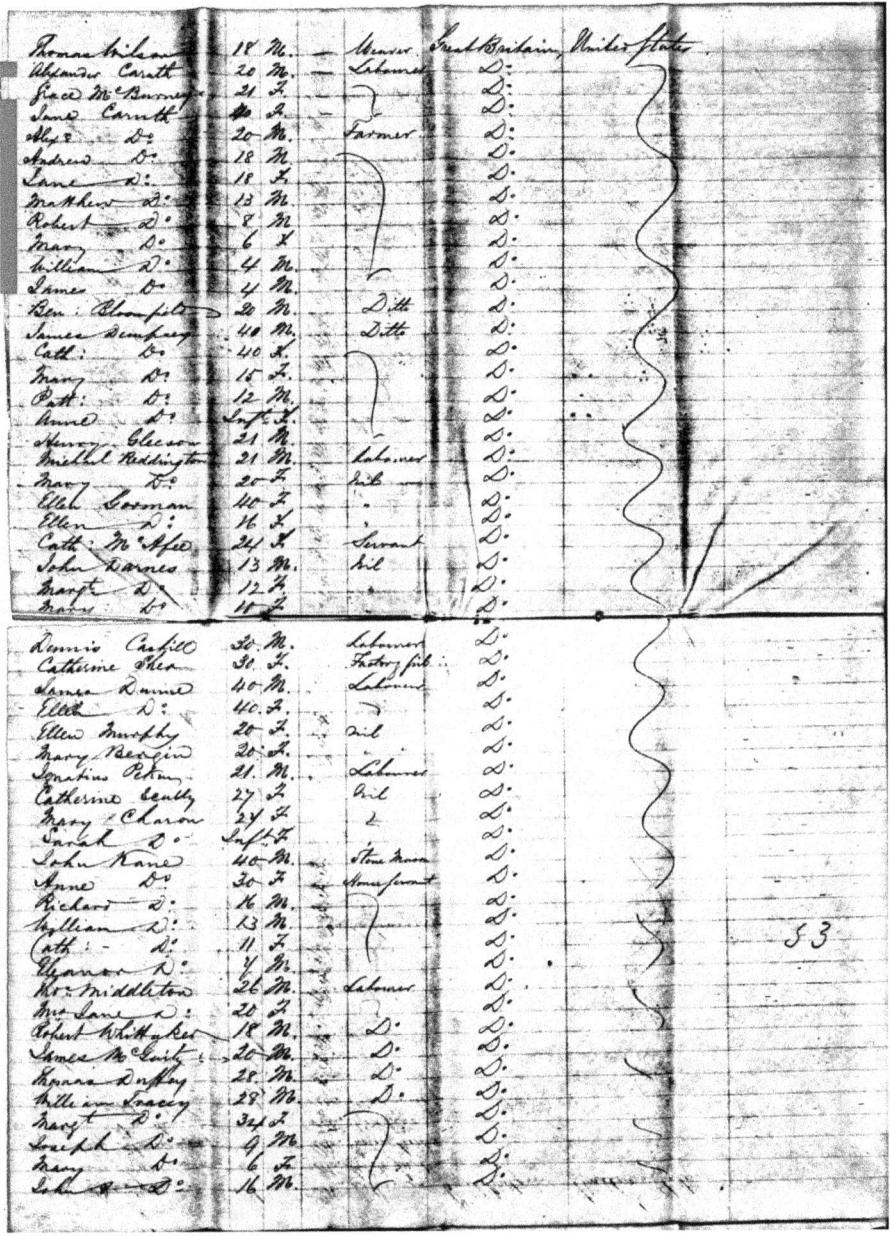

*12 September 1853 Passenger Manifest of the Enterprise: Liverpool to New York
National Archives Series m237, Roll 131, List 950, page 2*

This shows the Caruth Family's arrival in New York City

1870 Census: Andrew Caruth Household in Paw Paw Twp, Lee County, IL
National Archives Series m593, Roll 246, page 509a

1870 Census: Andrew Caruth Household in Paw Paw Twp, Lee County, IL
National Archives Series m593, Roll 246, page 509b

1870 Census: Alexander Caruth Household in Brooklyn Twp, Lee Cty, IL
National Archives Series m593, Roll 246, page 256

1880 Census: Andrew Caruth Household in Wyoming Twp, Lee County, IL
National Archives Series t9, Roll 225, page 451

1880 Census: Alexander Caruth Household in Wyoming Twp, Lee Cty, IL
National Archives Series t9, Roll 225, page 450

CARUTH BRANCH ANCESTRY

1900 Census: Thomas A. Caruth (w/Mary J. Caruth) Hhd in Wyoming Twp, Lee Cty, IL

My Grandsons' Caruth-side Ahnentafel Chart

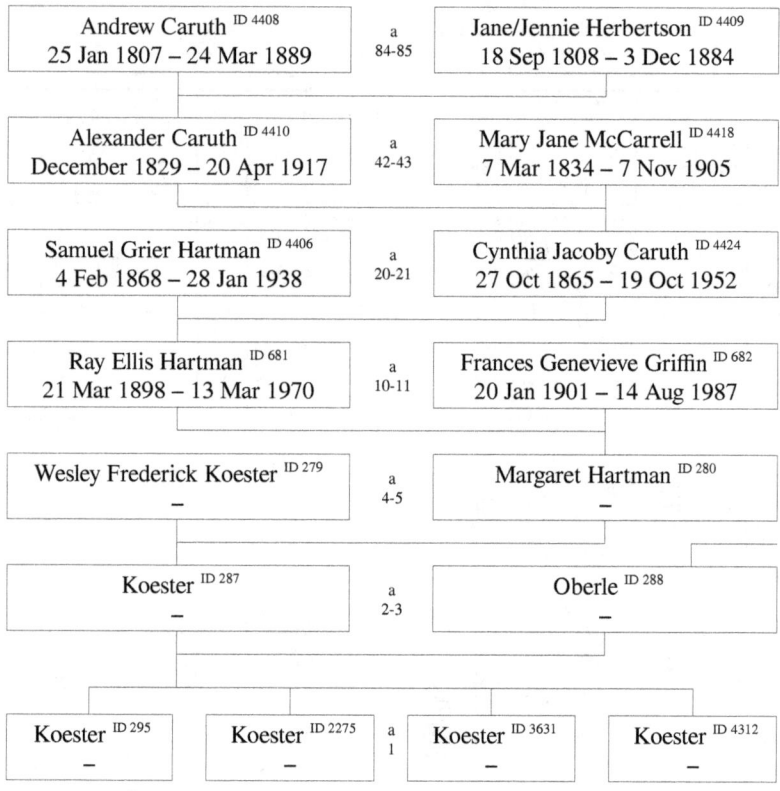

An Ahnentafel chart showing my Grandsons' Hartman-side is on page 46.

An Ahnentafel chart showing my Grandsons' Hunt-side is on page 102.

An Ahnentafel chart showing my Grandsons' Koester-side is on page 131.

Griffin Ancestry

According to the 1900 U.S. Census, your maternal grandparents Edward and Maggie (Hunt) Griffin were married in about 1898. At

> MY GRANDFATHER
> EDWARD FRANCIS GRIFFIN
> CLINTON TOWNSHIP, DEKALB COUNTY, IL.
> BORN - 5-24-1864
> DIED - ? -1936

the time, your grandfather would have been about 34 years old, and your grandmother about ten years younger. Your grandmother's ancestry is discussed in "Hunt Ancestry" beginning on page 87.

> MY GREAT GRANDFATHER
> PATRICK GRIFFIN
> DON'T KNOW
> BORN - 3-17-1816
> DIED - 8-5-1903

> MY GREAT GRANDMOTHER
> MARY ANN (GRAY) GRIFFIN
> DON'T KNOW
> BORN - 1-15-1831
> DIED - ?

In the 1900 U.S. Census (see page 83), Mary Ann's birth is reported as being in April of 1834, although the date you give (1-15-1831) seems to be more consistent with other data I've located – she would have only been 16 years old when she married if she were born in 1834, for instance – and is what appears on her headstone in St. James Calvary Cemetery. It was not at all uncommon, however, to encounter females whose reported ages show that they only aged six or seven years between the ten year census periods.

I haven't attempted to locate any generations earlier than Patrick and Mary Ann[32], whom you have already identified, but what other information I have located about your Griffin forebears is nothing if not confusing. I'll begin by saying that I strongly suspect that Patrick and Mary Ann were married in Ireland and had at least the first three of their children there before migrating to this country. Later comments by your grandfather Edward and his older brother William suggest, however, that their parents did not come from the same area of Ireland, leading to a possible clue as to where they each might have lived. Before discussing that (see "The Griffin's Origins Revisited" on page 69), however, it would be appropriate to discuss the mystery surrounding their immigration.

---

[32] In the first section of this book, I said that only the American history of your ancestors would be discussed.

Immigration

On the 1900 census (see page 83), Patrick Griffin says that he came to the U.S. from Ireland in 1855, at which time he would have been about 39 years old, and had been residing in this country for forty-five years. On the same form, his wife Mary Ann says she came from Ireland in 1858 when she would have been about 27, and had been residing in this country for forty-two years. It seems clear, therefore, that they did not travel to this country together. By itself, that isn't at all unusual for families in this period.

I have located two passenger manifests that seem to match these arrivals fairly well. The illustrations on pages 77 and 78 show a "Patt Griffin, age 40, Laborer" on the ship Lady Russell, which arrived in New York from Tralee[33], Ireland on 1 June 1857, then continued on to New Orleans. This is not, of course, a perfect match for Patrick, since it is two years off what he reported in 1900. Of the numerous other Patrick[34] Griffins who came to this country during that period, however, this is the only one that is close enough to be considered within the usual limits of error when someone reports his year of arrival to a census taker forty-five years after the fact. The Lady Russell was first commissioned in 1854, by the way, making it better than the average ship on which an Irish immigrant would travel in those days.

The illustrations on pages 79 and 80 show a "Mary Ann Griffin, age 27, from Ireland" on the ship Meridian, which arrived in Boston from Liverpool, England on 2 June 1857. This matches reasonably well to what Mary Ann reported in 1900, and is the only documented arrival I could locate that is even close to the particulars she provided. Like "Patt Griffin," she was unaccompanied on the journey.

I also searched for a Mary Ann Grady, but found no similar arrivals in the U.S. between 1855 and 1860.

Even if the records described above are not actually those of your great-grandparents, though, it remains likely that Patrick and Mary Ann certainly did not arrive together, and that they each arrived after 1855.

Now compare these arrival dates with the birth dates of their first three children. Their son William was born in April of 1852, their daughters Margaret and Maria were born in about 1853 and 1854 respectively[35]. It would therefore seem

---

[33] Tralee is the largest town in County Kerry, located in the far southwest of Ireland; the significance of this will be noted a little later.

[34] ... or Pats, Patts, Paddys, Padraighs, and the like.

[35] We see William's month and year of birth on the 1900 census (see page 83), and Margaret's and Maria's ages are shown on the 1870 census (see page 81) as 18 and 16 respectively. See the family diagrams on pages 75 and 76.

reasonable to assume that Patrick and Mary Ann must have been married in Ireland and that at least their first three children William, Margaret, and Maria were born there.

If Patrick then came to the U.S. alone (again – not uncommon in this period), got settled, and then sent for Mary Ann and their children, this could work out nicely. He would have left Ireland after Maria's birth.

The problem I have with this conclusion is that the censuses from 1870 through 1930 (see pages 81 through 86) all show William being born in the U.S., and the censuses of 1870 and 1880 likewise show Maria[36] as being born in America. Having incorrect origins listed for children of immigrants isn't all that unusual on census reports, but it seems like a stretch that it would be reported incorrectly over six censuses as it is in William's case. Of course, it has to be considered that Patrick and Mary Ann simply lied to the children about where they were born – this would not have been hard to understand. Looking at the 1900 census, it is clear that neither Patrick nor Mary Ann ever applied for naturalization[37], which would have made all of their minor children citizens. In the era before births were officially recorded, such a fib would permit the children to claim citizenship with little difficulty.

Even more troublesome is that, according to the 1900 census (see page 83), the fourth child Annie (by then called Anna Falk) was born in March 1857, implying that she must have been conceived in about June 1856. According to the immigration dates reported by Patrick and Mary Ann, he was supposedly in the United States in 1856 while Mary Ann was presumably in Ireland. Of course, if "Patt Griffin," who arrived in June of 1857, is actually Mary Ann's husband, this would work out well.

Given the age difference between Patrick and Mary Ann, it might seem that Mary Ann could possibly have been Patrick's second wife, and not the birth mother of the first few children, but the 1900 census shows that Mary Ann was the "mother of six, with five living" – thus seeming to rule out that possibility.

It is possible, of course, that one or both parents made multiple crossings but, if so, this would have been quite unusual for Irish immigrants of the time, which was a particularly tough period in Irish history; most never returned to their home country.

I have been unable to locate any trace of Patrick and Mary Ann's children in any passenger manifests or immigration records. I have also been unable to locate

---

[36] Margaret was also shown as born in Illinois in the 1870 census, but was not listed in the 1880 census, possibly because she was married by that time (she would have been 28 in 1880).

[37] We know this because column 18 of the census form is blank.

the family in the 1860 census anywhere in the United States. This raises another possibility, however, and that is that the family may actually have gone from Ireland to Canada. I haven't explored this, though, since their own statements seem to indicate that they came to this country directly. This might bear further exploration.

Patrick died on August 5, 1903 and, like Mary Ann, was buried in St. James Calvary Cemetery in Lee, DeKalb County, IL. Interestingly, the headstone doesn't include any death date for Mary Ann, nor was I able to locate any Illinois death records whose particulars came close to matching her data.

The Children of Patrick and Mary Ann Grady Griffin

See the diagram on page 75 when following this discussion. Listing the known children of your great-grandparents would seem to be a rather straightforward exercise but, again, examining the available information about Patrick and Mary Ann's children raises a number of interesting questions, the first of which has to do with the names and number of their children.

The table to the right shows the Griffin children as reported in the 1870 and 1880 censuses (see pages 81 and 82). These show the names of seven and six children respectively (with your grandfather Edward as the last), but the names and ages of the second-last child are different, leading me to suspect that they could possibly be the same person.

1870 (see pg 81)	1880 (see pg 82)
William, age 19	William, age 29
Margaret, age 18	
Maria, age 16	Maria, age 26
Annie, age 12	Annie, age 23
Patrick, age 10	Patrick, age 21
Charlie, age 8	John, age 20
Edward, age 6	Edward, age 16

The family makeup is further obfuscated by the statement on the 1900 census (see page 83) that Mary Ann was at the time the mother of six children, with five living. This leaves several questions: First, of course, was the sixth child's name John Charles, Charles John, or neither?

In an attempt to resolve the Charlie/John question, I searched through the 1900 census for eponymous men of the right approximate age who were living in Illinois, and located only two men named John Griffin and one named Charles Griffin. Although any of these might have seemed like reasonable matches otherwise, they all listed other states as their parents' birthplaces. So – the name of the second-last child will probably remain unknown unless you have some access to a family bible or find either of these names in a family cemetery plot.

A second, and more perplexing, question is: if Mary Ann was a "mother of six," why do there seem to be seven different names, even if we assume that Charlie and John are the same person? I'll suggest one possibility in a later section titled "The Family Farm" on page 70.

The third question is: Which child died before the 1900 census was taken?

- Since I could find neither of the names discussed above (Charlie or John) in the next available census, the sixth child, whatever its name might be, is certainly a possibility. We know that the oldest child William was living in your grandfather's household at least through 1930, so he isn't a candidate.
- Margaret, the second known child, only appears in the 1870 census, where she is reported to be 18 years old. She may have later married, explaining why her name didn't appear in 1880; even so, she could have married and died in childbirth, which would make it possible for her to be the deceased child.
- The third child, Maria, is a possibility. Maria was a 26 year old school teacher still living with her parents in 1880, and a notation on that census indicates that she had had one hand amputated. She could, however, also have married before 1900, which would explain why I could not locate her after 1880.
- The fourth child, Annie, had married Obadiah J. (Frank) Falk and had a son, Frank in June of 1892. By 1900, however, she and Frank were also living in your grandfather's household, so she is accounted for. She and Obadiah had possibly separated in the interim, since he didn't die until 1936[38].
- The fifth child, Patrick Griffin (Junior), also seems to be a good candidate, since I was unable to locate anyone of that name in Illinois. Once again, wandering some cemetery plots (or records) might be the best approach to determining which child died young.

The Griffin's Origins Revisited

I alluded earlier to your grandfather and his brother having made comments concerning their parents' origins. On the 1930 census (see page 86), both brothers list their father's origin as "Ireland, North" and their mother's as "Ireland, Free." It seems reasonable to assume that they must have lived in relatively close proximity in order to meet and get married (keep in mind that it is only my assumption that they were married in Ireland, but that seems to be supported by their own statements on the census forms). If so, this would imply that Patrick probably lived in Fermanagh, Monaghan, or Armagh County, and Mary Ann lived in Cavan or Louth County. The counties of Tyrone and Londonderry in Northern Ireland also border the northwest Ireland County of Donegal, but since these are all relatively close to the major emigration port of

---

[38] I should mention here that the 1890 census was totally destroyed by a fire in the early twentieth century, and there don't seem to be any surviving city directories for towns as small as those in which your ancestors lived.

Derry (Londonderry), it doesn't seem likely that they would have emigrated through Liverpool if they lived in the latter locations. This is simply speculation on my part, however.

The significance of "Patt Griffin" being listed as having come from Tralee on the Lady Russell's manifest now becomes apparent, since County Kerry is about as far as one can get from the Northern Ireland border and still be in Ireland. Although the Irish had a habit of making sure their Irish County was listed on their headstones, this isn't the case for either Patrick or Mary Ann.

The Family Farm

It is difficult to be certain from the census records, but it appears[39] that the Griffin family lived on the same farm continuously from at least 1870 through 1930 and presumably later. The value of the property was reported as $5,900 in 1870; compared to the other farms in the area, this was a little larger than the average. I suspect that the apparent ownership of the farm might provide a clue to the discrepancies in the number of children Mary Ann had reported on the 1900 census.

Your great-grandfather Patrick Griffin listed his profession as "farmer" in the 1870 and 1880 censuses, and as "landlord" in the 1900 census. At the time of the 1900 census, it appears that your grandfather Edward leased the property from his father Patrick, which would explain the "landlord" designation.

Edward F. Griffin, circa 1898

It seems somewhat unusual for the youngest child to be the head-of-household, particularly since the oldest brother, William, continued to live there and is listed as a "Farm Laborer" in Edward's household. William is clearly listed as Patrick's son in 1880 and as Edward's brother in all subsequent censuses. It was Edward, however, who seemed to have inherited the property after his parents' death[40]; William continued to be listed as part of Edward's household on the 1930 census, while Edward's sister Marguerite was living with him at the same location as late as the 1940 census.

This might suggest that William may not actually have been Mary Ann's son, explaining why she was

---

[39] If you scroll through the records, for instance, it is easy to spot some of the same names on the adjoining properties from decade to decade. I haven't attempted to locate any land records to verify this, however.

[40] DeKalb County records for deaths prior to 1916 have not yet been indexed

only reported to have had six children. Could William have been adopted and, if so, might he have been Patrick's son from an earlier marriage?

Patrick was almost fifteen years older than Mary Ann, so a previous marriage doesn't seem out of the question. This still wouldn't explain why William didn't receive the farm, however. It isn't difficult to come up with a number of reasons why Edward would have received the farm[41] but, since they would all be completely the work of imagination, they aren't worth repeating here.

Your Grandfather Edward's Date of Death

In your letter, you gave your grandfather Edward's year of death as being 1936. This would seem to be confirmed by the date carved into his tombstone (see image right).

The only death recorded for any Edward Griffin in Illinois in this period, however, was in Waterman Township, DeKalb County, on 13 November 1935[42] – reasonably close to 1936, but different enough to question. Death Certificates are known to have errors[43], but it is quite unusual for the date of death to be incorrect. Since the date is also quite specific, it may be that the year of death on his tombstone is incorrect.

Another interesting thing about your

Griffin Tombstone at St. James Cemetery in Lee

---

[41] ... ranging, of course, from the utterly benign to the deliciously scandalous ...
[42] His DeKalb County death certificate number is 0046620.
[43] The error rate seems to be about 29 percent according to Dr. Kenneth V. Iverson on page 21 of his book *Death to Dust – What happens to Dead Bodies?* Typically, however, the errors are found in the cause of death and age of the deceased.

grandfather we notice is that in 1870 and 1880, while he was living with his parents, his age was reported as 6 and 16 respectively, which is consistent with his birth date of 24 May 1864. Once he was married, however, he seems to have lost two years, and his age is given as 34, 44, 54, and 65 on the 1900, 1910, 1920 and 1930 censuses respectively.

On the 1900 census, which is the only one reporting month and year of birth as well as age, he gives his birth date as May 1866, rather than May 1864. There's probably a story there, but I can't tell what it might be or whether it is related to the discrepancy in his year of death.

The Children of Ed and Maggie Hunt Griffin

Maggie Hunt Griffin, circa 1898

I doubt very much if I could locate any information about your grandparents that you weren't already aware of, so I didn't attempt to go beyond the following.

Edward Francis Griffin and Margarette Hunt Griffin were married on 26 April 1898, eventually having five children, of whom your Mom Frances Genevieve was the second, born on 20 January 1901. Pictures of your Mom can be found on pages 8, 13, and 16.

The fifth and final child's gender isn't known; its existence can only be inferred from the statement on the 1900 census saying that Maggie is the "mother of 1 with 1 living" and the notation on the 1910 census saying that she is the "mother of 5 with 4 living." Therefore, another child must have been born and died between 1900 and 1910.

I mentioned your grandfather Ed's death certificate above; your grandmother Maggie died on 12 August 1920, just a few weeks after the 1920 census was taken. Her DeKalb County death certificate number is 0030580.

Suggestions for Further Research

To fill in more details about your Griffin ancestors, the following might prove useful:

- For various reasons, none of the many passenger manifests I've been able to locate so far are convincing matches for Patrick and Mary Ann Griffin. It might be helpful, therefore, to expand the search to include arrivals in Canada[44] during the period from about 1848 (when Patrick was about 32 and Mary Ann was about 17) through 1855.

- Determine the purchase date for the Griffin cemetery plot pictured above.

- Locate the Wills of Patrick or Mary Ann might help to determine William's status, and whether or not he was actually Mary Ann's son.

- Locate the grave of Edward and Margarette Griffin's infant or child who was born and died between 1900 and 1910; this could establish the name and gender of the child, which might in turn provide a starting point for determining the cause of death if that is considered genetically relevant. The grave does not seem to be located with the Griffin's graves in St. James Cemetery in Lee but might be located with Edward's parents' graves[45].

- Margarette Hunt Griffin was only about 45 years old when she died. It might be interesting to know her cause of death. The typical place to research this would be at the DeKalb County Courthouse, particularly since her death certificate number (0030580) is known.

---

[44] I did locate a Patrick Griffin in the 1861 Canadian Census for Montréal, Quebec, but he was born in 1821 and the particulars of his family don't match yours. I was unable to locate any other useful references in Canada's 1861 Census, but this likely doesn't mean much, since many of the Irish immigrants simply passed through to the United States without ever settling in Canada. Immigrants from Canada to the United States were not tracked until much later in the nineteenth century.

[45] Maggie Hunt's parents are buried in Iowa (see the Hunt Ancestry section) and there is no indication that there are any other burials in their plot. In any case, they seem to have moved to Iowa before this child would have been born.

Index of Illustrations Page

Griffin Ancestry Diagram 1 of 2 for Margaret Hartman Koester	75
Griffin Ancestry Diagram 2 of 2 for Margaret Hartman Koester	76
1 June 1857 Passenger Manifest of the Lady Russell: Liverpool to New York; National Archives Series m237, Roll 174, List 598, page 1; Title Page of Manifest (truncated for legibility)	77
1 June 1857 Passenger Manifest of the Lady Russell: Liverpool to New York; National Archives Series m237, Roll 174, List 598, page 5 (w/ "Patt Griffin"), age 40 (ergo YOB=1814 – good match)	78
2 June 1857 Passenger Manifest of Meridian: Liverpool to Boston; National Archives Series m277, Roll 50, page 1; Title Page of Manifest	79
2 June 1857 Passenger Manifest of Meridian: Liverpool to Boston; National Archives Series m277, Roll 50, page 8; Griffin (Mary Ann Griffin) (Good match but there are no children.)	80
1870 Census: Patrick Griffin Household in Clinton Township, DeKalb County, Illinois; National Archives Series m593, Roll 215, page 352 (with Edward as a child)	81
1880 Census: Patrick Griffin Household in Clinton Township, DeKalb County, Illinois; National Archives Series t9, Roll 202, page 15 (with Edward as a child)	82
1900 Census: Patrick and Edward Griffin Households in Clinton Township, DeKalb County, Illinois; National Archives Series t623, Roll 296, page 21	83
1910 Census: Edward Griffin Household in Clinton Township, DeKalb County, Illinois; National Archives Series t624, Roll 284, page 21	84
1920 Census: Edward Griffin Household in Clinton Township, DeKalb County, Illinois; National Archives Series t625, Roll 302, page 234	85
1930 Census: Edward Griffin Household in Clinton Township, DeKalb County, Illinois; National Archives Series t626, Roll 510, page 5a	86

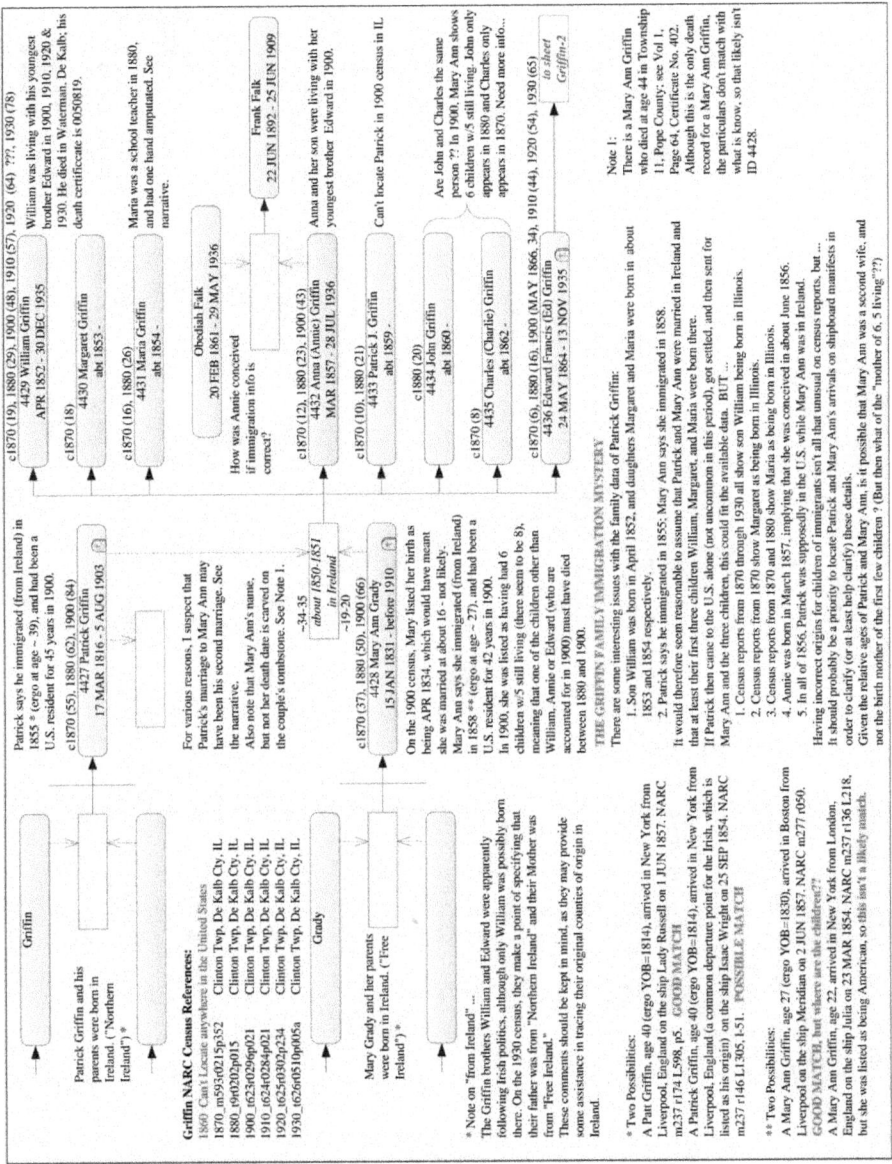

Griffin Ancestry Diagram 1 of 2 for Margaret Hartman Koester
The "Griffin-2" reference from Ed Griffin points to the diagram on page 76.

Hartman – Koester Ancestry

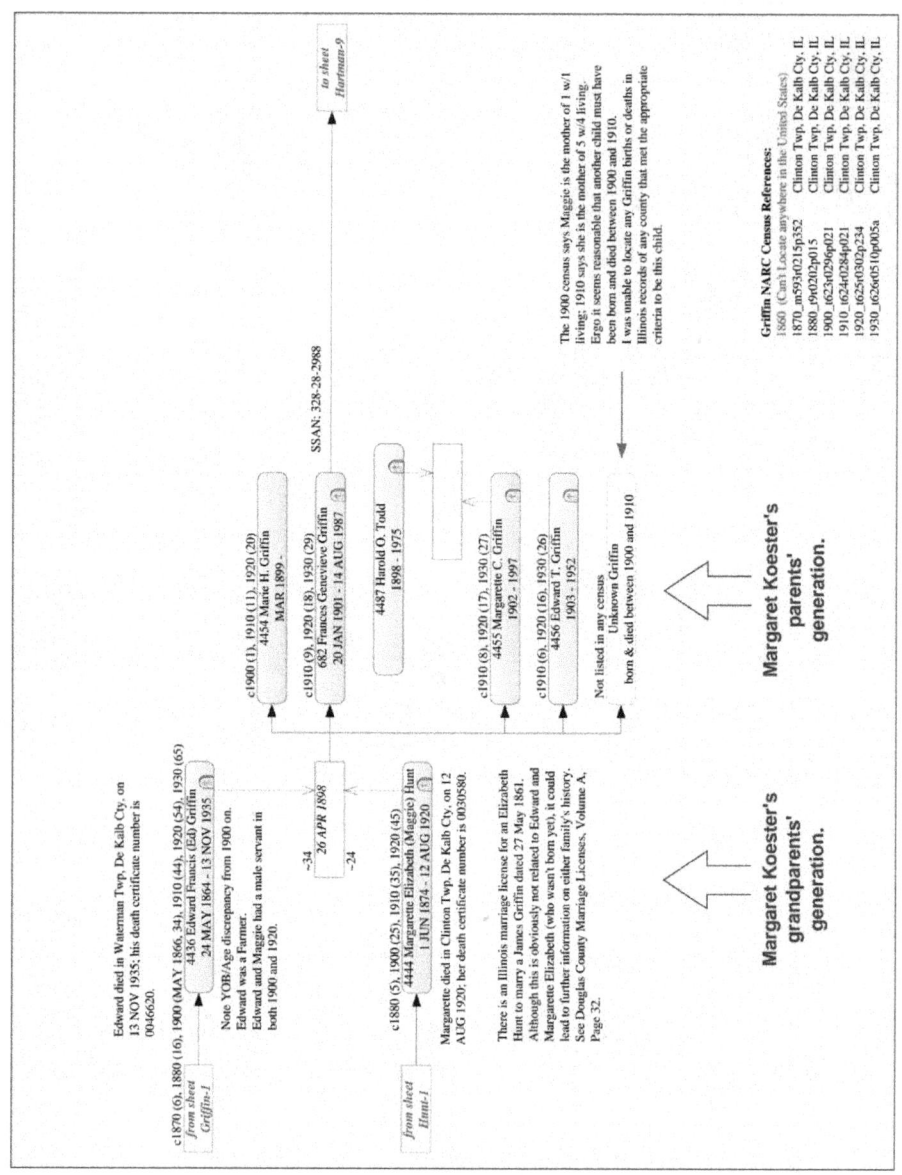

Griffin Ancestry Diagram 2 of 2 for Margaret Hartman Koester (Griffin-Hunt)
The "from Griffin-1" reference pointing to Ed Griffin comes from page 75
The "from Hunt-1" reference pointing to Maggie Hunt comes from page 92.
The "to Hartman-9" reference from Frances Griffin points to the diagram on page 21.

1 June 1857 Passenger Manifest of the Lady Russell: Liverpool to New York
National Archives Series m237, Roll 174, List 598, Title Page
Bottom of page truncated for legibility

1 June 1857 Passenger Manifest of the Lady Russell: Liverpool to New York National Archives Series m237, Roll 174, List 598, page 5, with Patt Griffin, age 40 Bottom of page truncated for legibility; Passenger 211 is the closest match for Patrick Griffin located in contemporary passenger arrival manifests.

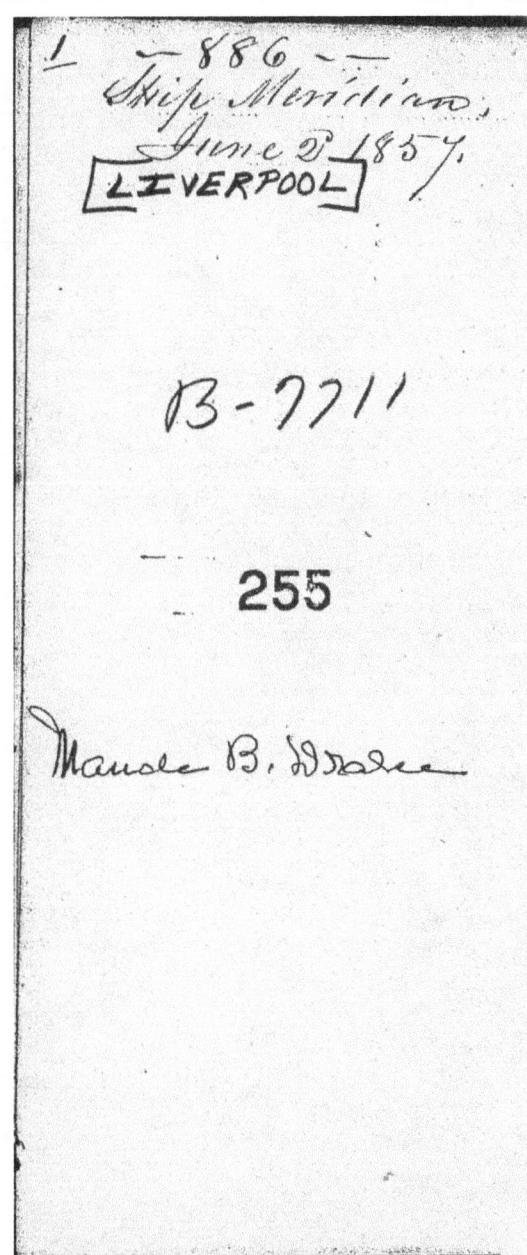

2 June 1857 Passenger Manifest (cover) of Meridian: Liverpool to Boston; National Archives Series m277, Roll 50, page 1; Griffin (Mary Ann Griffin)

NAMES	AGE	SEX	Occupation, Trade, or Profession	Country to which they severally belong	
Mary Foley	16	F	Unstated	Ireland	
Ellen Haverty	16	"	"	"	
Denis Nolan	18	M	"	"	
Ann Robinson	37	F	"	"	
Mary "	2	"	"	"	
Caroline "	Infant	"	"	"	
Mary Shear	Unstated	"	"	"	
Ellen Peach	40	"	"	"	
Patk "	20	M	"	"	
James "	10	"	"	"	
Margt "	8	F	"	"	
Ellen Ronane	19	"	"	"	
Margt "	15	"	"	"	
Cath Connors	33	"	"	"	
Patk Devine	26	M	"	"	
Ann "	28	F	"	"	
Andrew "	6	M	"	"	
Robert Nelson	21	F	"	"	
Maria Clayton	23	"	"	"	
Martin Rogan	30	M	"	"	
Mary O'Donnell	20	F	"	"	
Mary Baley	23	"	"	"	
Ann Connelly	17	"	"	"	
Margt Faherty	28	"	"	"	
Margt "	7	"	"	"	
Mary Ann Griffin	27	"	"	"	
Bdgt Connor	18	"	"	"	
James Robinson	22	M	"	"	
Patk McElray	20	"	"	"	
Benj McDermott	32	"	"	"	
Cath Flinn	30	F	"	"	
Jno Connolly	Unstated	M	"	"	
Cath "	"	F	"	"	
Bdgt Mack	16	"	"	"	
Patk Bradley	32	M	"	"	
David Smith	33	"	"	"	

2 June 1857 Passenger Manifest of Meridian: Liverpool to Boston
National Archives Series m277, Roll 50, page 8; Griffin (Mary Ann Griffin)

1870 Census: Patrick Griffin Household in Clinton Twp, DeKalb County, IL
National Archives Series m593, Roll 215, page 352

*1880 Census: Patrick Griffin Household in Clinton Twp, DeKalb Cty, IL
National Archives Series t9, Roll 202, page 15*

The eight members of the Griffin household are listed in the last eight lines.

*1900 Census: Edward & Patrick Griffin Households in Clinton Twp, DeKalb Cty, IL
National Archives Series t623, Roll 296, page 21*

1910 Census: Edward Griffin Household in Clinton Twp, DeKalb Cty, IL
National Archives Series t624, Roll 284, page 21

GRIFFIN BRANCH ANCESTRY

1920 Census: Edward Griffin Household in Clinton Twp, DeKalb Cty, IL
National Archives Series t625, Roll 302, page 234

As in 1880, the eight members of the Griffin household are listed in the last eight lines.

1930 Census: Edward Griffin Household in Clinton Twp, DeKalb Cty, IL
National Archives Series t626, Roll 510, page 5a

Hunt Ancestry

On 6 May 1862, Edmund and Julia Hunt of Ireland, both aged 50, left the port of Liverpool, England on the ship S.S. Neptune with their Johanna, age 17, Thomas, age 15, and William, age 7. They arrived at the port of New York on 28 May. Although not certain, a search of available records indicates that Edmund and Julia are most likely your 2nd great grandparents, and Thomas your great-grandfather. I have been unable to locate any trace of either Edmund or Julia after their arrival in the United States in either census or death records, but on the 1900 U.S. Census (see page 98), Thomas reports that he emigrated from Ireland in 1861, when he would have been about 16 years old.[46]

> *MY GREAT GRANDFATHER*
> *THOMAS HUNT*
> *MAYBE IRELAND*
> *BORN - ?*
> *DIED - ?*

The next year, on 5 October 1863, Margaret Hunt, age 55, Bridget, age 16, and Owen, age 15, also left Liverpool on the S.S. Frances A. Palmer, arriving on 27 October 1863. These also seem to be your relatives, but not your direct ancestors. At the time of the 1870 census (see page 96), both Margaret and Owen were living with your great-grandfather Thomas and his wife Henrietta (known as Etta) in Northville Township in La Salle County, Illinois. It can be speculated that Margaret is either Edmund's older sister, but since she is traveling with two teenagers, it is more likely that she may be the widow of Edmund's brother.

The family arrived just as the Civil War was imminent, so I checked military records for the period. There were eight Union soldiers (but no Confederates) from Illinois named Thomas Hunt who were all infantrymen, but none of them seem to match your great-grandfather's particulars. Furthermore, I was unable to locate any match in the record of Union Army pensioners either, leading to the conclusion that Thomas was never in the military.

It appears, however, that Owen joined the Navy as a "soldier," which in the context of the time would be what we now call a marine. Since he would only have been about fourteen years old at the end of the Civil War, though, it is likely that he joined after that conflict was over. He was stationed at the Norfolk Navy Yard at the time of the 1880 census, but I was unable to locate him after that.

---

[46] A common European custom was to state ages as ordinal rather than cardinal numbers; thus a one year old child was in its first year, while an American child wasn't considered one year old until it had lived for one year. Reported ages of immigrants often vary.

The Dreishmeyer Family

I was unable to locate any records with the spelling "Dreishmeyer," but several records that match what is known of the family appear under spellings that range from Driefmeyer to Dietmer.

> *MY GREAT GRANDMOTHER*
> *HENRIETTA (DREISHMEYER) HUNT*
> *DON'T KNOW*
> *BORN - ?*
> *DIED - ?*

Etta Dreishmeyer Hunt didn't indicate any origin for her parents on the 1880 census (see page 97), but on the 1900 census (see page 98), she says that her father was born in Germany and her mother in Illinois. In 1910 and 1920, however (see pages 100 and 101), she says both of her parents were German.

Henrietta/Letty/Etta would have been about seven years old in 1860, and since she claims to have been born in Illinois, her parents must have been in this country before then. The most likely match for the family's arrival is shown on pages 93 and 94, where "Hry Driefmeyer"[47] and his wife Mary, both aged 38 (implying a birth year of 1809±2), and their five children arrived in New York on the "Bremen Ship Emma" on 25 October 1847 from Bremen. The children ranged in age from 3 to 15 years old.[48]

Assuming this is Henrietta's family, this is not inconsistent with the Oct 1851 month and year of birth she reports on the 1900 census. It therefore seems reasonable to speculate that Henry and Mary are your 2nd great-grandparents, although the fact that I can't locate the family in any census record is troubling.

The Children of Thomas and Etta Dreishmeyer Hunt

According to the 1900 U.S. Census shown on page 98, your great-grandparents Thomas and Henrietta Hunt were born in October 1844 and October 1851 respectively. The couple was married on 17 March, 1870 in Illinois when he was about 25 and Etta/Letty about 19. As mentioned earlier, the 1870 census lists Thomas, Etta, and Owen in Margaret Hunt's household (Thomas' Aunt?). Although the 1870 census didn't ask for relationships of each person in the household to the head of the household, we know that Etta is, in fact, Thomas'

---

[47] Since Henry is obviously German, it is tempting to assme that perhaps the "f" in "Driefmeyer" is actually an "ſ," indicating their name might actually be "Drie*ss*meyer." There is, in fact, a family headed by Henry Dreismeyer (whose wife is named Mary) living in Illinois at the time of the 1860 census, but their ages are 33 and 29 respectively.

[48] Caspar, 3 (b.~1844); Ann, 4 (~1843); Wilhelmina, 6 (~1841); Adam, 13 (~1834); and John, 15 (~1832).

wife because that census does have a column (14), marked "If married within the year, state month." These are completed with "Mar" for Thomas and Etta.[49]

Their marriage in DeKalb County is recorded in Volume D, page 84 of the Illinois state archives, where her name is given as Dreishmeyer, Letty.

Thomas and Letty Hunt had at least thirteen children, of which your grandmother Maggie was the third child and second daughter. See the diagram on page 92 for details of their family.

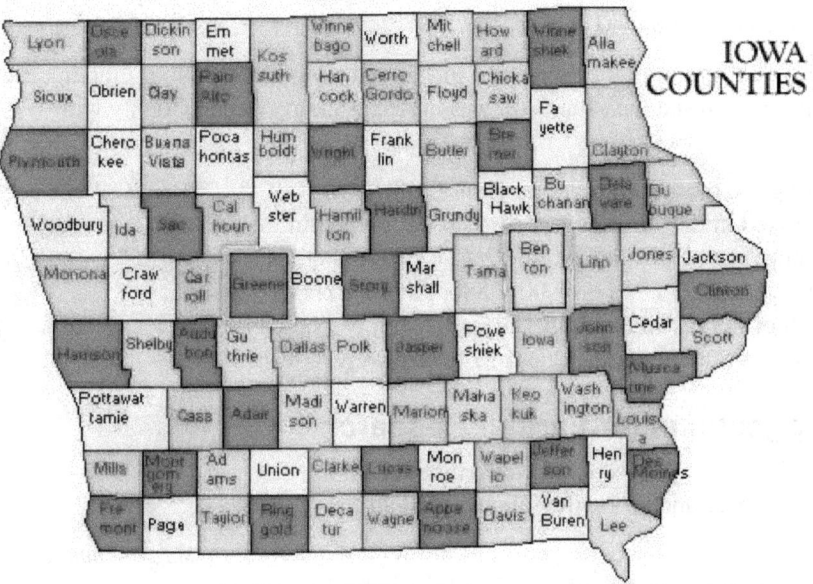

IOWA COUNTIES

By 1880 (see page 97), their first five children, including your grandmother, had been born, and the family was living in the town of Somonauk in DeKalb County. They remained in Illinois at least until February 1892 when their last son Arthur was born. It is likely that they continued to live in Illinois until your grandmother Margarette Elizabeth Hunt married Edward Griffin in about 1898, but they must have relocated their family to Iowa shortly thereafter. By the time of the 1900 census (see pages 98 and 99), they were living there in Cedar Township, Greene County, with their ten remaining children. By 1910, they had moved again to Highland Township in the same county. Their son David, who was not living with them in 1900, was now back in the household with a son of his own, suggesting that he may have been married and lost his wife in that ten-year span.

---

[49] Looking closely, it can be seen that the census taker originally checked box 13 ("born within the year"), but then crossed these marks out and marked box 14.

Your great-grandfather Thomas died in 1914, and is buried in section 23 of St. Patrick's Cemetery in Churdan, Cedar Township, Greene County, Iowa.[50] Greene County is located a little west of central Iowa, and is the left of the two counties highlighted on the map to the right.

Etta continued to live in Iowa, and at the time of the 1920 census (see page 101) had her household in Vinton Township, Benton County, with one of her daughters, her son-in-law[51], and three grandchildren. Benton County is five counties to the east of Greene County, and is marked on the map on county map provided on the previous page.

Your great-grandmother Etta died in 1937, having outlived your grandmother[52] by more than sixteen years, and was buried back in Greene County with Thomas.

Your grandmother Margarette Hunt Griffin, who is discussed in the "Griffin Ancestry" section, died in Clinton Twp, DeKalb Cty, on 12 AUG 1920; her death certificate number is 0030580. Another photograph of her, as well as a picture of her tombstone are in that section on pages 72 and 71 respectively.

Suggestions for Further Research

To fill in more details about your Hunt and Dreishmeyer ancestors, the following might prove useful:

Maggie (Hunt) Griffin

- Continue searching for United States immigration records or passenger manifests (including those to Canada). The manifest would likely be in 1861 (± 1), and include the following:

  ♦ an Adult Male (optional, since we don't know if the family left after the father died or not)

  ♦ an Adult Female named Margaret or some variant, age about 62 (± 1)

  ♦ a Son Thomas, age about 17 (± 1), born October 1844

  ♦ a Son Owen, age about 10 (± 1), born October 1851

  ♦ possibly other children

---

[50] This information is courtesy of the first President Obama (FDR) who set the WPA to making lists of the burials around the country; this section of Iowa was serendipitously included in that effort before it was ended, and the lists are public record.
[51] ... although Albert is listed as "brother-in-law" rather than "son-in-law" for some reason.
[52] ... who was Etta's second oldest daughter.

- Locate the grave of your 2nd great-grandmother Margaret Hunt (born abt 1799 and died between 1870 and 1880), last known to have lived in Northville Township in LaSalle County. This would enable you to confirm her years (and perhaps dates) of birth and death. Knowing whether her husband is buried with her would establish whether he came to the United States with the family in the early 1860s and died in the intervening decade, or died before the family emigrated to this country. The Irish immigrants of that period often list their Irish Counties of origin, so that might provide further clues to assist in locating some trace of them in Irish records.

Index of Illustrations   Page

Hunt Ancestry Diagram for Margaret Hartman Koester	92
25 Oct 1847 Passenger Arrival Manifest of "Bremen Ship Emma" (1) for the family of "Hry Driefmeyer"; National Archives Series m237, Roll 69, page 925	93
25 Oct 1847 Passenger Arrival Manifest of "Bremen Ship Emma" (2) for the family of "Hry Driefmeyer"; National Archives Series m237, Roll 69, page 926	94
28 May 1862 Passenger Arrival Manifest of the Neptune for the family of Edmund and Julia Hunt; National Archives Series m237, Roll 219, page 336	95
1870 Census: Margaret Hunt Household (w/Thomas, Etta & Owen) in Northville Township, LaSalle County, Illinois; National Archives Series m593, Roll 244, page 466b	96
1880 Census: Thomas Hunt Household in Somanauk Township, DeKalb County, Illinois; National Archives Series t9, Roll 202, page 199	97
1900 Census: Thomas Hunt Household in Cedar Township, Greene County, Iowa; National Archives Series t623, Roll 433, page 2b	98
1900 Census: Thomas Hunt Household in Cedar Township, Greene County, Iowa; National Archives Series t623, Roll 433, page 3a	99
1910 Census: Thomas Hunt Household in Highland Township, Greene County, Iowa; National Archives Series t624, Roll 403, page 8a	100
1920 Census: Etta Hunt Household in Vinton Township, Benton County, Iowa; National Archives Series t625, Roll 477, page 259	101

HARTMAN – KOESTER ANCESTRY

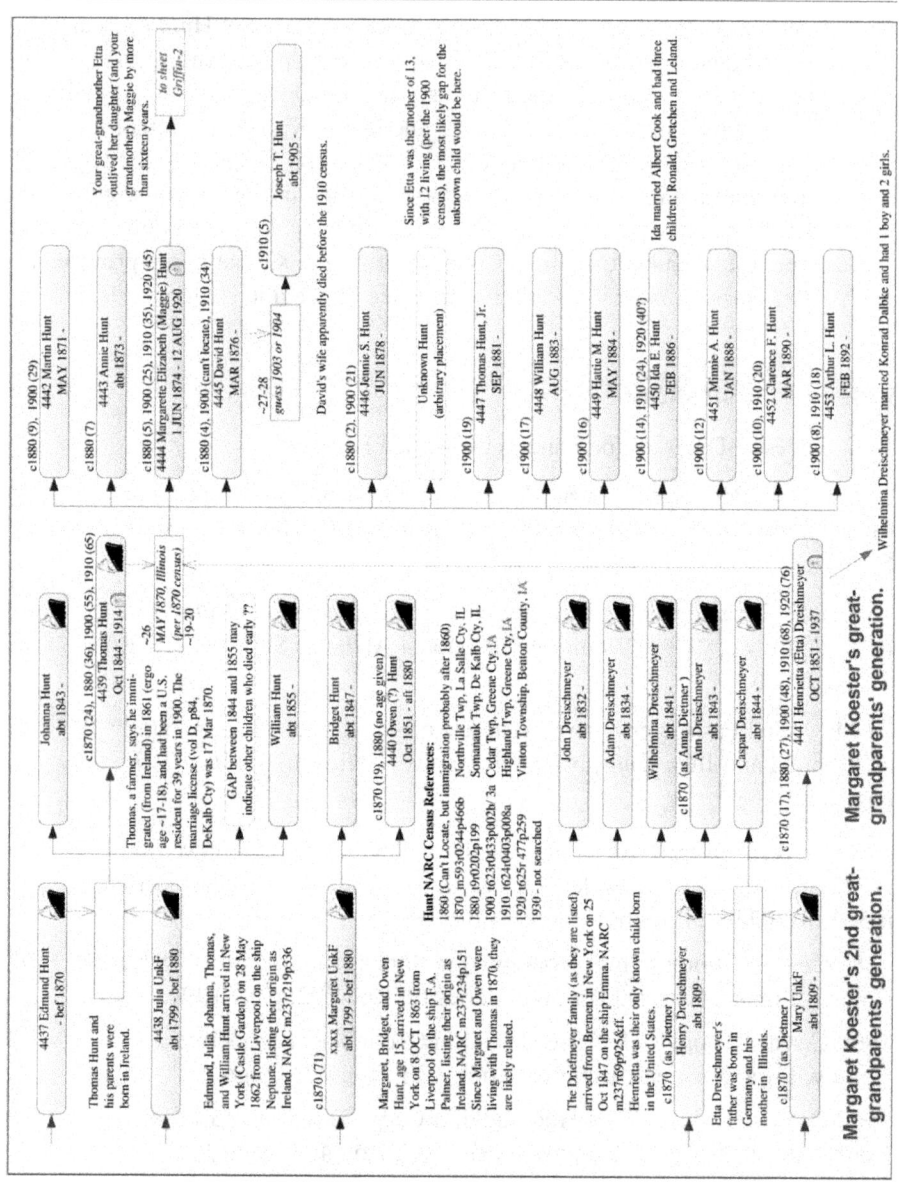

Hunt Ancestry Diagram 1 of 1 for Margaret Hartman Koester
The "to Griffin-2" reference from Maggie Hunt refers to the diagram on page 76

25 Oct 1847 Passenger Arrival Manifest of "Bremen Ship Emma" (1)
National Archives Series m237, Roll 69, page 925

Henry and Mary "Dreifmeyer" are passengers 119 and 120 on the last two lines.

25 Oct 1847 Passenger Arrival Manifest of "Bremen Ship Emma" (2)
National Archives Series m237, Roll 69, page 926

The remaining five "Dreifmeyers" are passengers 121 through 125 on the top lines.

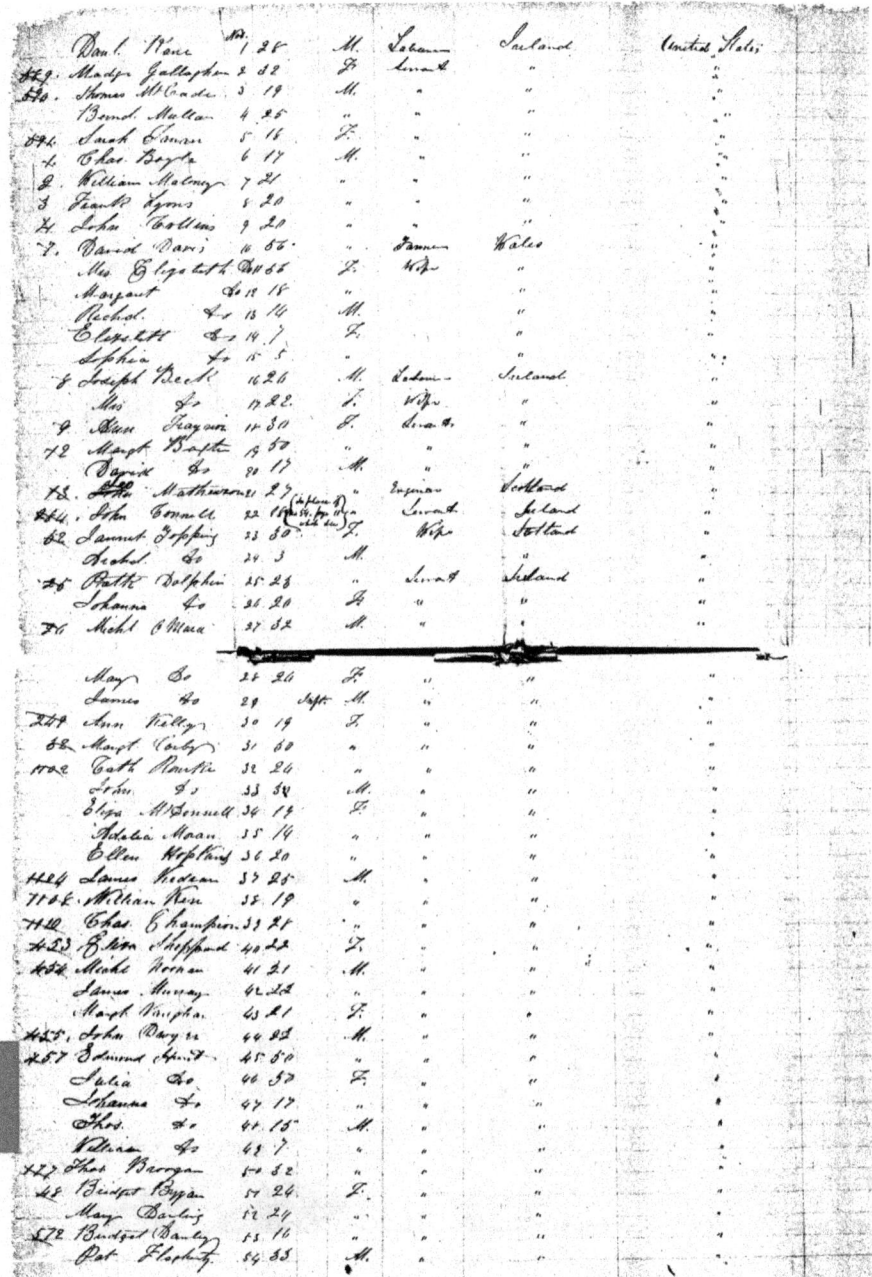

28 May 1862 Passenger Arrival Manifest of the Neptune
National Archives Series m237, Roll 219, page 336

Edmund Hunt and his family arrive in the United States

1870 Census: Margaret Hunt Hhd (w/Thomas & Etta) in Northville Twp, LaSalle Cty, IL
National Archives Series m593, Roll 244, page 466b

1880 Census: Thomas Hunt Household in Somanauk Twp, DeKalb Cty, IL
National Archives Series t9, Roll 202, page 199

1900 Census: Thomas Hunt Household in Cedar Twp, Greene Cty, Ia
National Archives Series t623, Roll 433, page 2b

1900 Census: Thomas Hunt Household in Cedar Twp, Greene Cty, Ia; National Archives Series t623, Roll 433, page 3a

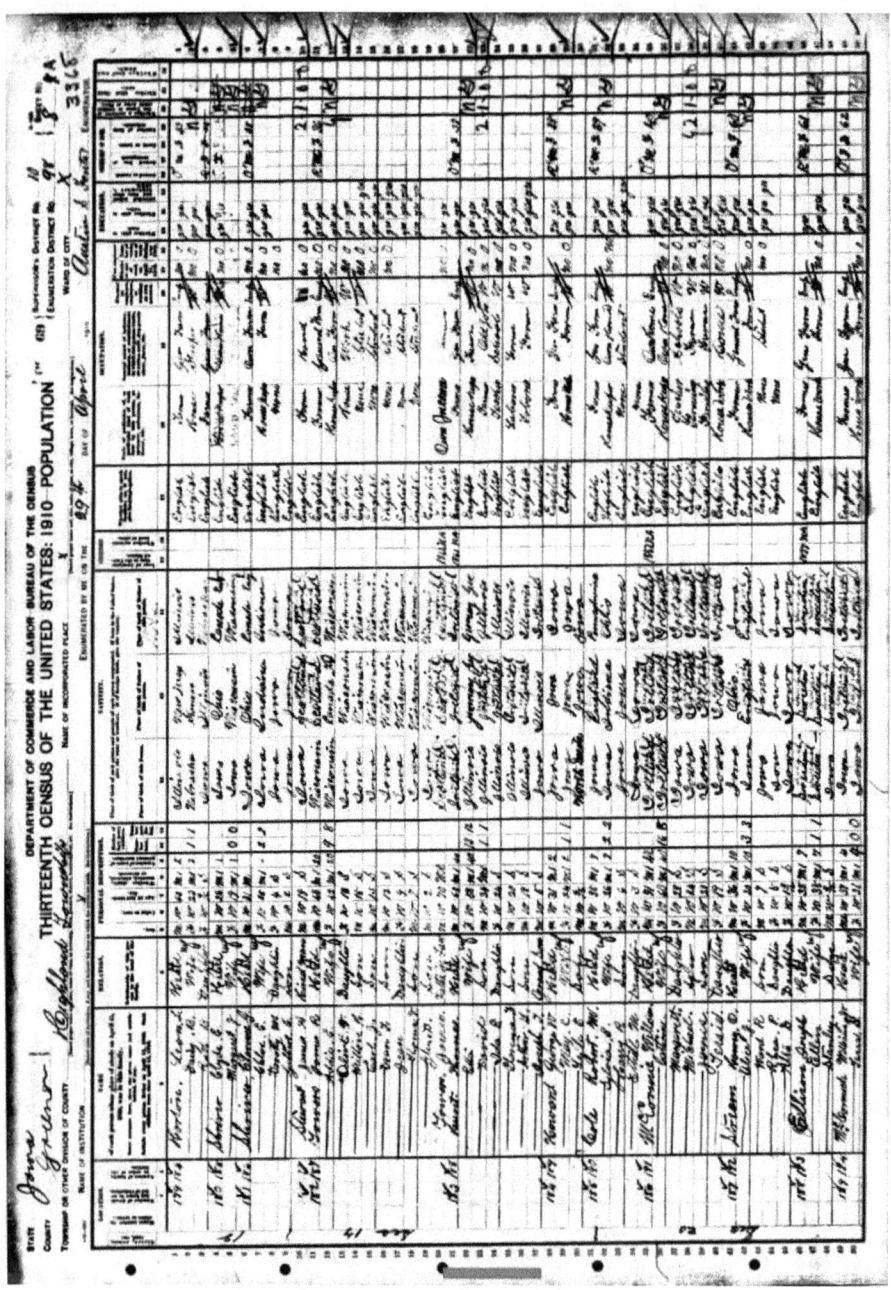

*1910 Census: Thomas Hunt Household in Highland Twp, Greene Cty, Ia
National Archives Series t624, Roll 403, page 8a*

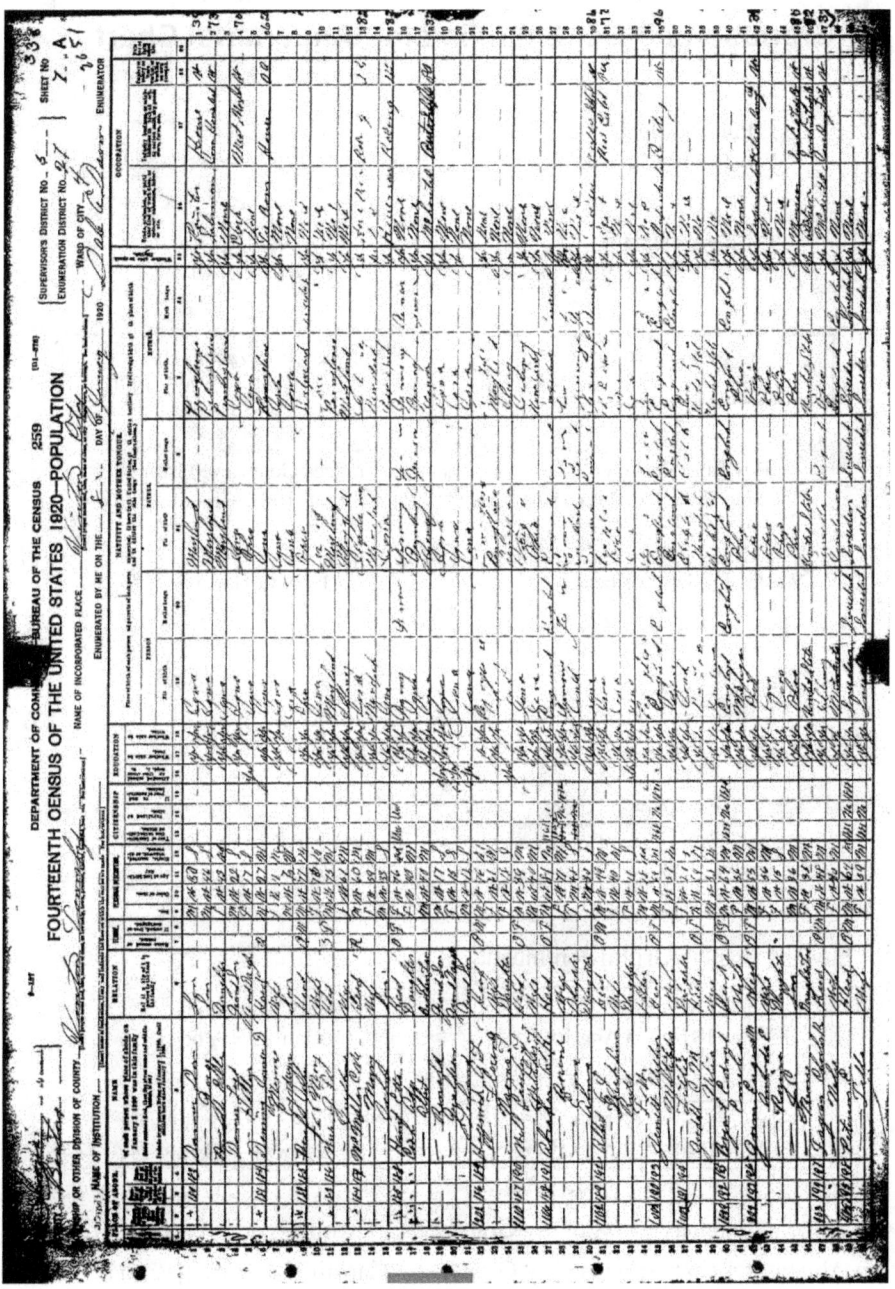

*1920 Census: Etta Hunt Household in Vinton Twp, Benton Cty, Ia;
National Archives Series t625, Roll 477, page 259*

My Grandsons' Hunt & Griffin-side Ahnentafel Chart

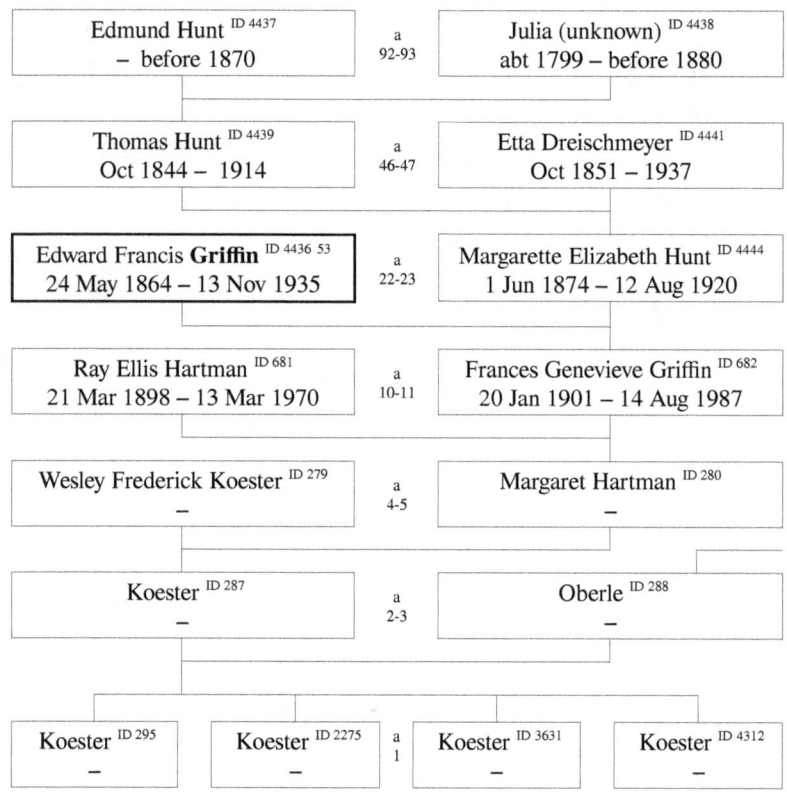

... Edward Francis Griffin continued:

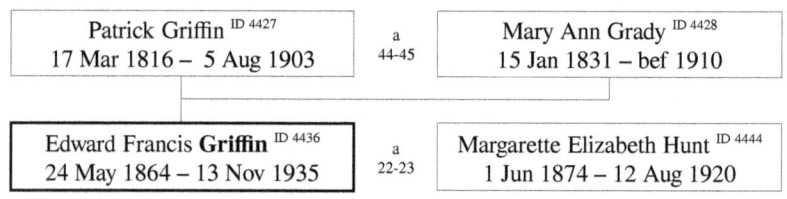

An Ahnentafel chart showing my Grandsons' Hartman-side is on page 46.
An Ahnentafel chart showing my Grandsons' Caruth-side is on page 64.
An Ahnentafel chart showing my Grandsons' Koester-side is on page 131.

---

[53] A continuation of Edward Griffin's parents is shown immediately below.

Koester Ancestry

The Koester Name and Family

The original German form of the name was "Köster" or "Küster," and both variants can be found in the very few Germanic records[54] known to be connected to the family's forebears. The name itself likely refers to some early Küster's role as a church "sexton." Since English has no umlaut, the name adopted by the family upon settling in the United States became either Koester (to preserve the sound) or, less frequently, Koster (simply dropping the umlaut). Alternatively, some "Kösters" acquired their name from their family origins near Kösten, Germany.[55] Depending on the specific context, any of several variant spellings may be used within this chapter.

When I was a child growing up in Baltimore, Maryland, the bread everyone in our neighborhood ate was Koesters[56] Twin Bread, delivered to our back doors by one of the drivers of the company, which was founded in 1886 by Eilert (1858-1948) and his wife Lisette (1860-1947) Koester. Like the Koesters discussed in this short history, they both were born in Germany. Since at least one of my Koester grandsons is a baseball fan and player, it is interesting to mention that, in its earlier days, the Koester Bakery had also issued baseball cards with their bread – a practice usually only associated with chewing gum producers. As it happens, a 1921 Babe Ruth card from the company[57] is one of the more valuable baseball cards ever traded.

So, unlike many of the surnames in my own ancestry which were unfamiliar to me until I began tracing my distant family history, I've known the Koester name all my life. My next encounter with the name came later – I left the military on

---

[54] Many historic vital records from the Ostfriesland region were destroyed during World War II by allied bombing of the key North Sea port regions near Bremerhaven, Emden, etc.
[55] This does not likely apply to your family, since Koesten is east of Berlin – a fair distance from Jever and Friesland.
[56] ... although it was always pronounced "Kester" there.
[57] One of these sold for over $10,000; the set itself is D383 in the American Card Catalog.

my birthday in November 1978 when my daughter (now a Koester) was barely 7 years old; by December I had accepted a position in Escondido, California with a small group of people that had relocated from Oak Industries of Crystal Lake, Illinois, to establish a new division in California. The president of the division (and my boss's boss) was a man named Werner Koester and, although he divided his time between Illinois and California, the staff in Escondido was small enough that we all got to know each other reasonably well. Later, after my subsequent transfers to Phoenix and Chicago with the company, I was generally the one who picked up Werner at the airport during his visits, since I was one of the few people in the new operations he knew.

Werner was an entertaining story teller once he became comfortable with whatever group he was in. He had gotten his pilot's license at a very young age and, during World War II, flew many combat missions. Occasionally, however, newcomers would become confused by these tales. One afternoon, a group of us, including a new engineer, John, who knew nothing of Werner's history, were listening to stories about his wartime aerial experiences. John began to look increasingly confused by the details Werner was recounting; finally, when the light struck him, John said none too tactfully: "Oh!! You were the *Enemy*!!"[58] Everyone else knew, of course, that Werner had flown for the Luftwaffe – not emigrating to the United States until after the war.

Many years later, my daughter introduced our family to the person who would eventually give her a new surname. It wasn't until some years later, after my daughter had given me and her mother-in-law the "genealogy bug" (I suspect that Margaret was already afflicted, and only required a slight prod to come clean) that I saw their family's copy of "The Koster Family Album" which is reproduced beginning on page 133.

While browsing through the album one afternoon during a family get-together at my daughter's house, I was quite surprised to come across my old boss's photo on page 44 (reproduced on page 157 in this book) – quite a bit younger than when I knew him – but clearly the same man; when I asked, my son-in-law's father said that he had never met Werner, even though the two had lived in reasonably close proximity in Illinois for many years. The two were actually fourth cousins whose common ancestors, discussed below, were their 4th great-grandparents Otto Johannsen Kuster and Wobke Gerdes, who lived at the end of the eighteenth century.[59] This relationship is, of course, a pointless coincidence, but I'm amused easily enough that I found it interesting and worth mentioning.

---

[58] In his later years, a reporter interviewed Werner about his life. Although this interview, at has a mistake (he didn't retire in 1961 as the article states), it gives a flavor of the man. See *http://www.cdapress.com/lifestyles/article_ea48e641-e379-54d9-a59d-1ea1ff495e95.html*

[59] Otto and Wobke are introduced on page 105.

A Brief History of the Koester Line

JOHANN JOHANNSEN KUSTER ID 1328 AND HIS UNKNOWN WIFE

My grandsons' earliest confirmed Köster/Koster/Küster/Kuster/Koester ancestor is their eighth great-grandfather Johann Johannsen Küster ID 1328, who we know from extant records must have been born before 1615. The ancestral line from this Johann to my grandsons can be followed in the "My Grandsons' Koester-side Ahnentafel Chart" on page 131.

More information on each of my grandsons' Koester ancestors is available in "The Koster Family Album" which begins on page 133; details about Johann can be found on page 3 of that album (page 136 of this book).

A map showing the location of many German/northern European place names referred to in this book is provided on page 112.

We know virtually nothing about Johann, including the name of his wife, nor the number of children they may have had. We can safely surmise from his middle name Johannsen, however, that his father, like the three generations that followed him, was likely also named Johann.

JOHANN JOHANNSEN KUSTER ID 1332 AND MARIA HENRICHS ID 1333

Johann Johannsen Kuster ID 1332 (1631 – 31 Mar 1701) married Maria Henrichs ID 1333 (1649 – 31 Aug 1680), the daughter of Henrich Eylers ID 1329 of Updorf, on 20 May 1675. See the reference to "The Koster Family Album" above.

My grandsons' seventh great-grandparents are known to have had at least three children, of whom the oldest was yet another Johann Johannsen Kuster.

JOHANN JOHANNSEN KUSTER ID 1334 AND METKE HERMANNS BOSE ID 1337

Johann Johannsen Kuster ID 1334 (1676 – 27 May 1742) married Metke Hermanns Bose ID 1337 (27 Jan 1768 – 31 Jan 1728), daughter of Hermann ID 1330 and Metke Bose ID 1331. Metke's parents were buried respectively on 12 Feb 1709 and 31 Jan 1721.

Johann and Metke Kuster had seven children, of whom the sixth was Otto Johannsen (still "Johann's son," but no longer named Johann[60]), the direct ancestor – a fifth great-grandfather – of my grandsons.

OTTO JOHANNSEN KUSTER ID 1343 AND WOBKE GERDES ID 1347

Otto Johannsen Kuster ID 1343 (1 May 1716 – 17 Aug 1785) married Wobke Gerdes ID 1347 (27 Jun 1723 – 26 Jan 1803) in Blersum on 21 Jul 1746.

---

[60] As would be expected at the time, Otto's oldest brother, the third of Johann and Metke's children, received that name. Note the "sen" suffix, more Dutch than the German "son."

Wobke's parents – and one set of my grandsons's sixth great-grandparents – were Gerd Frerks [ID 1345] and Inse Folkerts [ID 1346]. Nothing is known of Gerd, but his wife Inse lived from 13 Oct 1698 to 23 Nov 1788.

HERMAN JOHAN KUSTER [ID 1361] AND MINELT GERDES [ID 1366]

Herman Johan Kuster [ID 1361] (26 Oct 1759 – 9 May 1806) married Minelt Gerdes [ID 1366] (7 Feb 1767 – ??), daughter of Gerd [ID 1429] and Ette Henrichs, on Jan 6, 1793, in West Schlepperhausen[61]. The first of their three children was my grandsons' 3rd great-grandfather Otte Janssen Kuster.

Note that Herman's bride had the same surname as his mother's. The relationship between the two Gerdes women is unknown, but given the size of the town, they were likely related. Information about Herman appears on page 5 of "The Koster Family Album," reproduced on page 137 of this book.

OTTE JANSSEN KUSTER [ID 1305] AND ANNA KATHERINA OSTERKAMP [ID 1306]

Otte Janssen (note the variant form of Johannsen) Kuster [ID 1305] (23 Aug 1793 – 10 Mar 1855) married Anna Katherina Osterkamp [ID 1306] (9 Sep 1802 – ??), daughter of Folkert Hinrichs Osterkamp [ID 1385] and Rienelt Hicken [ID 1386], on 23 Apr 1825 in Blersum. The last of their five known children was Folkert Otten Koester. This generation was the first instance where the spelling "Koester" was used that I'm aware of in this branch. For more details about Otte, see page 5 of "The Koster Family Album," reproduced on page 138.

FOLKERT OTTEN KOESTER [ID 1302] AND MEMARICH SANDERS [ID 1390]

Folkert[62] Otten Koester [ID 1302] (21 Mar 1845 – 1 Apr 1887) married Memarich (known as Marie) Sanders [ID 1390] (14 May 1849 – unknown), the widow of Siebelt Kellman. The couple – my grandsons' 2nd great-grandparents – had four children: the first two born in Jever and the youngest two born in Rahrdum.[63]

The third of these children, Boike Anton (called Anton), along with his youngest brother Johann [ID 1304] (born in 1883) were the first of the Koesters to migrate to the United States, arriving on the S.S. Oder on 9 May 1884; the passenger manifest page showing the brothers can be seen on page 116.

Folkert appears on page 66 of "The Koster Family Album," which is reproduced on page 168 of this book.

---

[61] The reference to West Schlepperhausen appears in the Koster Family Album, but I was only able to identify this as a street name, not a town or district. Hmmm...

[62] This name sometimes appears as Volguard rather than Folkert.

[63] Rahrdum is today considered a part of Jever, which is located in Friesland, Weser-Ems, Niedersachsen. Interestingly, two other branches of my own family come from Emden and Oldenburg, which are about equidistant (southwest and south-south-east respectively) from Jever.

KOESTER ANCESTRY

BOIKE ANTON KOESTER ID 678 AND IDA BRUNS ID 679

As mentioned above, Anton[64] Koester ID 678 (31 Mar 1876 – 9 Jul 1946), shown below in uniform, then just 18[65], and his 16 year old brother Johann left home together, traveled to Bremen, and boarded the S.S. Oder in April 1884. From there, the ship sailed to Southampton in England, before proceeding across the Atlantic to New York. The brothers' arrival at the port there on May 9th is recorded in the passenger manifest shown on pages 115 and 116.[66]

Some time later, having established himself in Iowa as a brewer, he returned to Rahrdum. On 11 May 1909, Anton left once again for the United States on the S.S. Kronprinzessin Cecilie. The page from the Cecilie's Passenger Manifest documenting Anton's arrival back in the United States is shown on pages 117 (the left side) and 118 (the right side, showing his destination to be LeMars, Iowa). The 1910 U.S. Census sheet on page 119 shows that Anton was then living with and working as a servant on the farm of John Eilers in Grant Township in Plymouth County, Iowa. At some time between then and early 1914, Anton Koester once again returned to his homeland, and there, on 16 May 1914, married Katherina Bruns ID 1392, the oldest of fourteen children of Wessel Mamme Bruns ID 1126 and Tatje Klasina Behrends ID 1127.

Anton, then 38, brought his 19 year old bride to Iowa with him, arriving in New York with her on the S.S. Grosser Kurfürst on 3 June 1914. Page 8 of the Passenger Manifest for the S.S. Grosser Kurfürst is shown on pages 120 and 121. Anton accompanied Katherina to Plymouth County, Iowa, which can be seen in the upper left of the map on page 89.

The S.S. Grosser Kurfürst

Their first child, a son named Freddie (per his birth record[67]), was born 11 March 1916; later that year, on September 28 1916, Anton (and therefore his

---

[64] The name Boike, a diminutive of Boye, is a Dutch-German nickname meaning "little boy."
[65] See footnote 46 on page 87. Because of the practice of using ordinal ages, it is quite possible that the brothers were only 17 and 15 years old respectively by our reckoning.
[66] As with other passenger manifests, the first page is reproduced to show the ship's information as well as the column headers for the remaining pages.
[67] His birth was recorded in Sioux City, Iowa, although he was likely born on their farm.

wife and son) became a naturalized citizen at the LeMars courthouse. A year later, on 21 September 1917, their second child Dorothea was born.

By this time, World War I had begun, and the Selective Service Act initiating the draft was passed the previous May. Anton's date of birth required him to register for the draft on 12 September 1918 and, at age 42, he did so. His draft registration card (see page 122) tells us that he was 5' 4" tall, with a medium build, grey eyes, and light brown hair.

By November of 1918, the Spanish Flu epidemic had reached LeMars. Anton's wife Catherine[68] succumbed to the disease on the ninth and, as was the practice during the epidemic, was buried by the following day. The next day Freddie, then age 2, died as well.[69] Coincidentally, this was the date the armistice with Germany was signed. Freddie and his mother are buried in Riverside Cemetery in Akron (Plymouth County) Iowa.

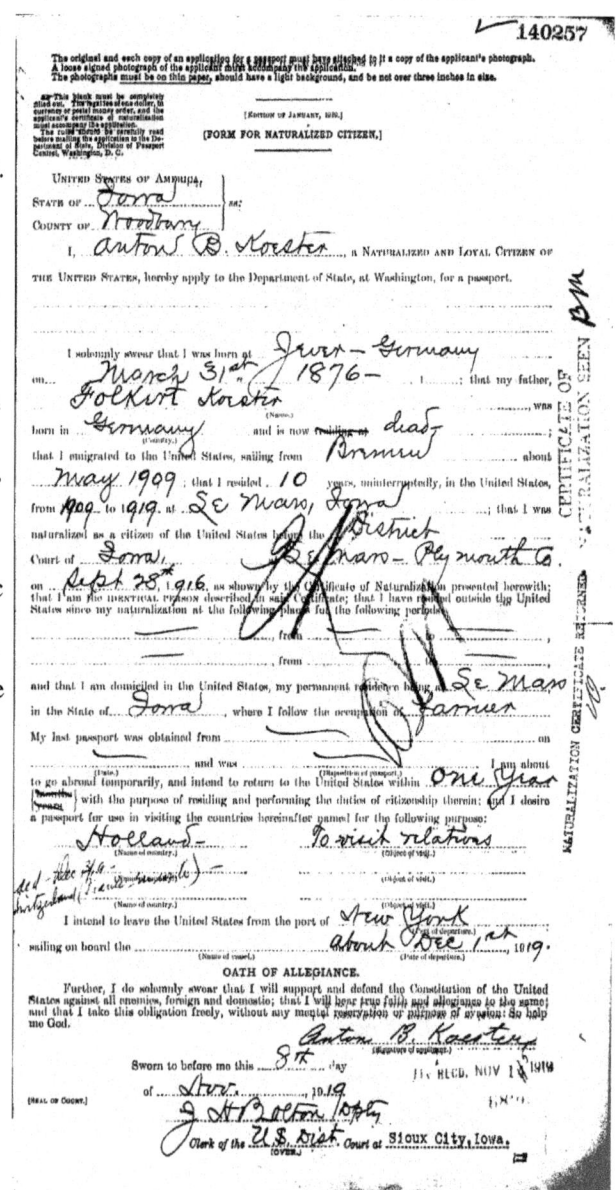

---

[68] The Iowa death records show the name Catherine; it was not uncommon for immigrants to change the spelling of their names to what they perceived to be "Americanized" versions.

[69] Their death records can be found in "Iowa Deaths and Burials, 1850-1990," available as the Family History Library microfilms 1,412,141 and 1,412,142.

The following November, after the formal Treaty of Versailles ending World War I had been signed on 28 June 1919, Anton applied for a U.S. passport (shown above) to return to Europe, stating that he intended to depart in December and return within a year. Although we know his family was still in Jever, he listed his intended destination as Holland rather than Germany.

Anton and his daughter Dorothea then left the United States and returned to visit his and Katherina's family. Before very long, though, on 20 June 1920, Anton had married Katherina's sister Ida Annette [ID 679] (30 Nov 1894 – 1968), the Bruns' second child.

While in Jever, Ida had two daughters: Irene [ID 1398] (born 28 May 1921) and Wilma [ID 1399] (born 16 Sep 1922), but post-war conditions in Germany were becoming increasingly harsh, making migration to the U.S. increasingly attractive.

In 1923, therefore, Anton returned to the United States, arriving in New York on the 29th of April on the S.S. President Fillmore. See sheet 138 of the Fillmore's passenger manifest on page 123. After establishing himself in Sterling, Illinois, he sent for his family.

Ida Annette Bruns at age 18

Anton and Ida Koester in 1938

Ida followed Anton in August – coincidentally, on the same ship as Anton had traveled – accompanying Dorothea (Katherina's daughter) and her own daughters Irene and Wilma. The left and right sides of the arrival manifest page are reproduced on pages 124 and 125.

Interestingly, the ship arrived in New York harbor on Friday the 3rd of August 1923, but was unable to dock at Ellis Island that day due to the high number of vessels attempting to discharge their passengers before the August immigration quotas were met.

At 7:30 pm that same day, President Warren G. Harding died unexpectedly in San Francisco. By the next morning, the entire country was aware that Vice-President Calvin Coolidge had been vacationing at his home in Vermont – which had no electricity or telephone service – and it wasn't certain by press time that he was even aware that he was now president. The result of this was uncertainty throughout the federal apparatus. Although the Ellis Island facility did not close completely, the delays were such that Ida and her daughters had to remain on board the S.S. Fillmore until the 6th, when Harding's funeral had taken place and the bureaucracies returned to normal.

Ida, Irene, and Wylma were naturalized in late 1923. After a few years, Anton and Ida had their first child in the United States, a son named Werner Volmar [ID 1400], who lived for only seven weeks until his death on 23 May 1927 in Jordan Township, Whiteside County.[70]

By 1930, the census (see page 126) tells us that the family was now renting a farm in Jordan Township in Whiteside, Illinois, with another German immigrant as a farm laborer.

Anton's sixth child – Ida's fourth – and my grandsons' "other" grandfather – was born in 1933. Wes can be seen on the 1940 U.S. Census sheet shown on page 128, with the rest of the family on the previous sheet, shown on page 127. The family was then living in Palmyra Township, in Lee County, Illinois

Anton died on 9 July 1946 at a little over 70 years of age. Ida lived until 1968, when she was 72. The couple is buried together at the Riverside cemetery in Sterling, Illinois.

Some additional anecdotal information about Anton and Ida's family can be found in some notes that Wes (pictured to the right) collected some years ago in a scrapbook he kept, and which are reproduced on pages 129 and 130.

Anton, Wes, and Ida Koester in 1940

---

[70] Werner Volmar Koester's Illinois death certificate number is 0980137.

Index of Illustrations   Page

Map of North Sea Coast showing Koester's Ancestral Areas	112
Bruns Ancestry Diagram 1 of 1 for Wesley Koester	
Koester Ancestry Diagram 4 of 5 for Wesley Koester	
9 May 1884 Passenger Manifest for the S.S. Oder; pg 1; National Archives Series m237, Roll 476, List 517.	115
9 May 1884 Passenger Manifest for the S.S. Oder; pg 2; National Archives Series m237, Roll 476, List 517. Anton and John Koester arrive in the United States.	116
11 May 1909 Passenger Manifest for the S.S. Kronprinzessin Cecilie; left side; National Archives Series t715, Roll 1262, Page 164	117
11 May 1909 Passenger Manifest for the S.S. Kronprinzessin Cecilie; right side; National Archives Series t715, Roll 1262, Page 164	118
1910 U.S. Census showing Anton Koester in Grant Twp, Plymouth Cty, Ia; National Archives Series t624, Roll 418, Page 5b	119
3 June 1914 Passenger Manifest for the S.S. Grosser Kurfürst; left side; National Archives Series t715, Roll , Page 8	120
3 June 1914 Passenger Manifest for the S.S. Grosser Kurfürst; right side; National Archives Series t715, Roll , Page 9	121
12 September 1918: World War I Draft Card for Anton Boicke Koester	122
29 April 1923 Passenger Manifest for the S.S. President Fillmore; left side; National Archives Series t715, Roll 3288, Page 138	123
6 August 1923 Passenger Manifest for the S.S. President Fillmore; left side; National Archives Series t715, Roll 3345, Page 151, L5	124
6 August 1923 Passenger Manifest for the S.S. President Fillmore; right side; National Archives Series t715, Roll 3345, Page 152, L5	125
1930 U.S. Census showing Anton Koester family in Jordan Twp, Whiteside Cty, IL; National Archives Series t626, Roll 566, Page 3b	126
1940 U.S. Census showing Anton Koester family in Palmyra Twp, Lee Cty, IL; Sheet 11a: showing Anton, his wife Ida, and their daughter Wilma; National Archives Series t627, Roll 836, Page 849	127
1940 U.S. Census showing Anton Koester family in Palmyra Twp, Lee Cty, IL; Sheet 11b: showing Anton and Ida's youngest son Wesley at age 7; National Archives Series t627, Roll 836, Page 850	128
Two summary pages of Koester Family History Notes from Wesley Koester's Scrapbook.	129, 130
My Koester Grandsons' Ahnentafel Chart	131

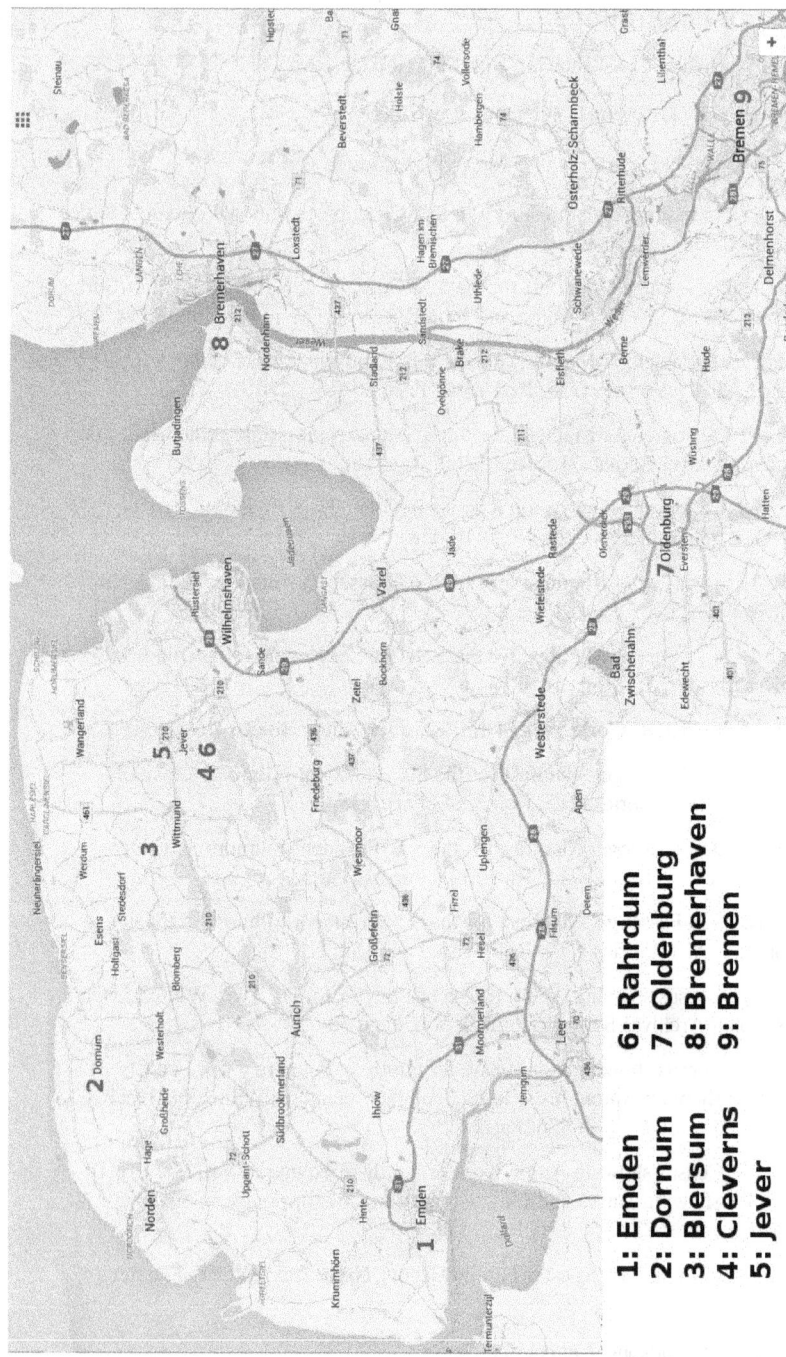

Map of North Sea Coast showing the Koester family's European Ancestral Areas

KOESTER ANCESTRY

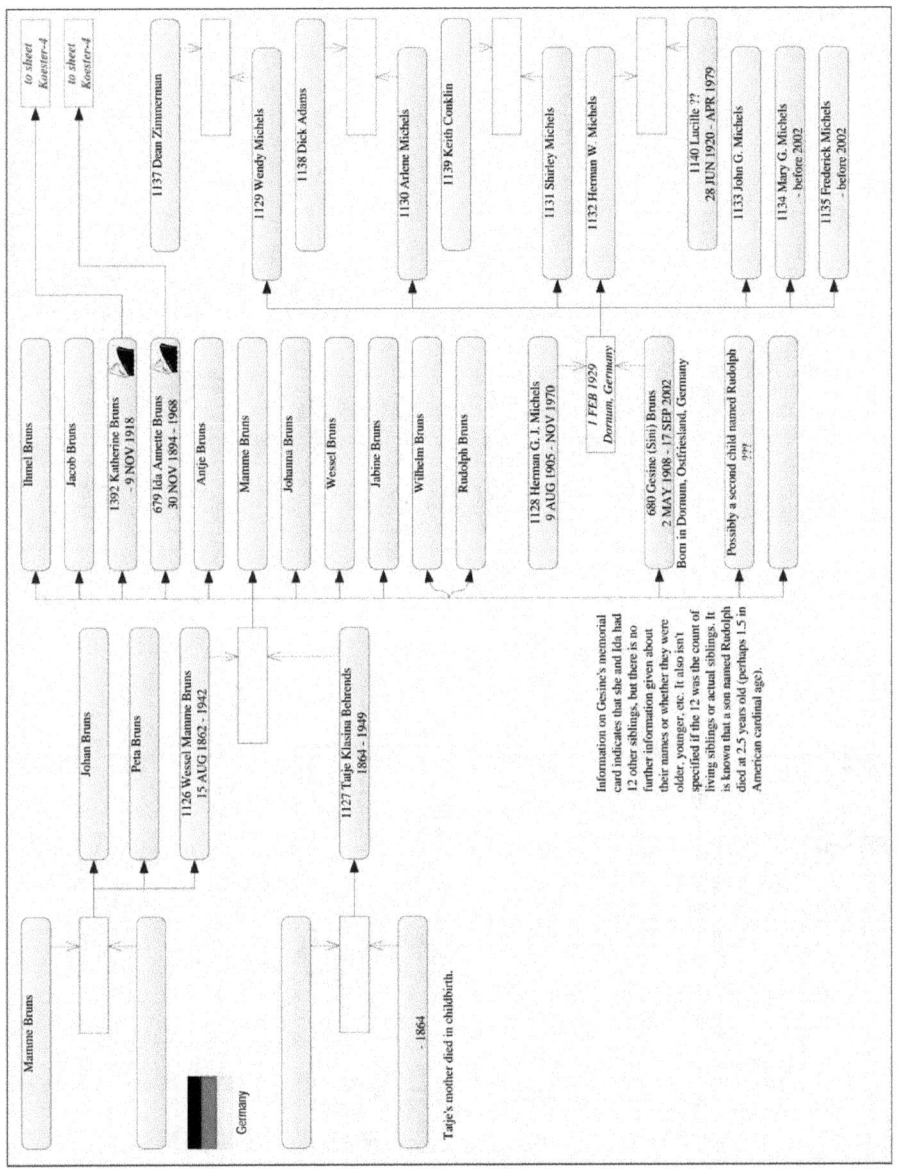

Bruns Ancestry Diagram 1 of 1 for Wesley Koester
The "to Koester-4" references from Katherine and Ida Bruns refer to the diagram on page 114

Hartman – Koester Ancestry

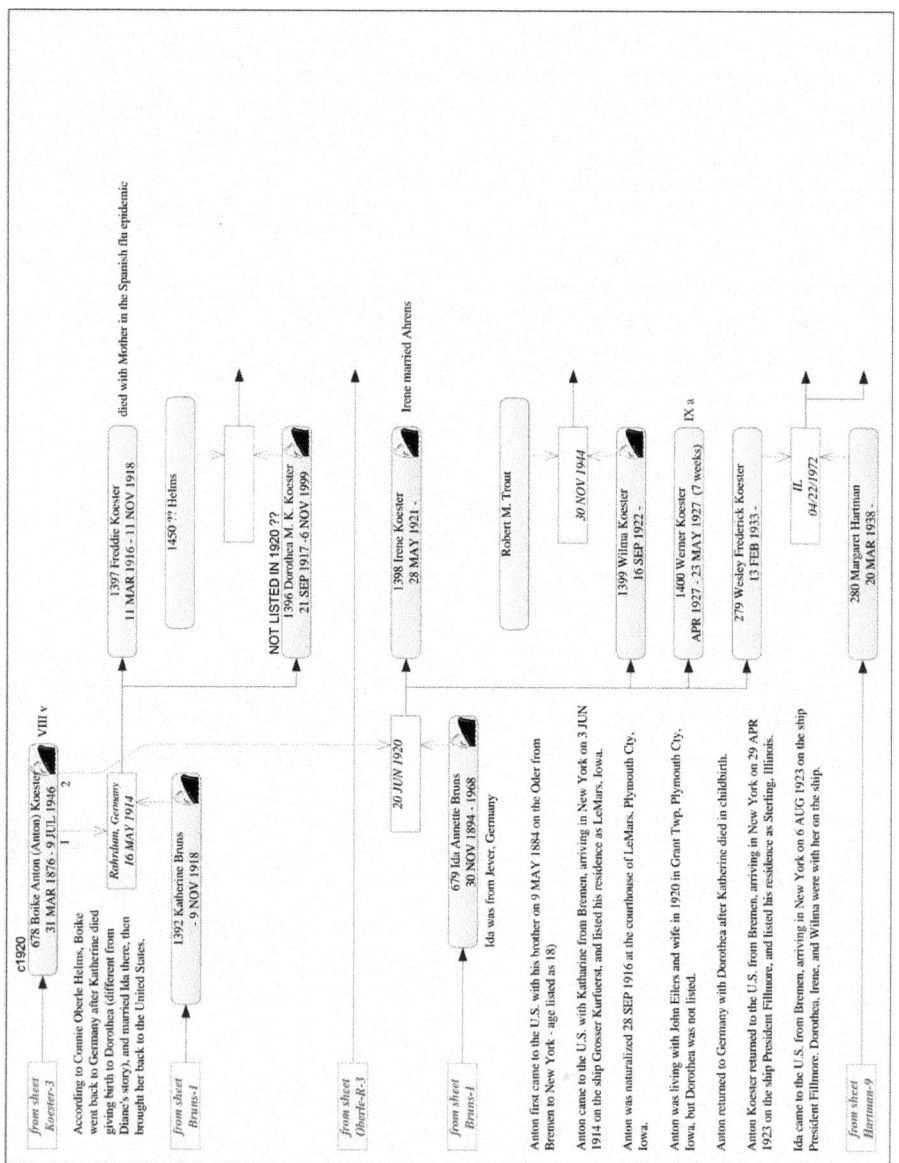

Koester Ancestry Diagram 4 of 5 for Wesley Koester
The "from Bruns-1" references pointing to the Bruns sisters comes from page 113.
The "from Hartman-9" reference pointing to Margaret Hartman comes from page 21.

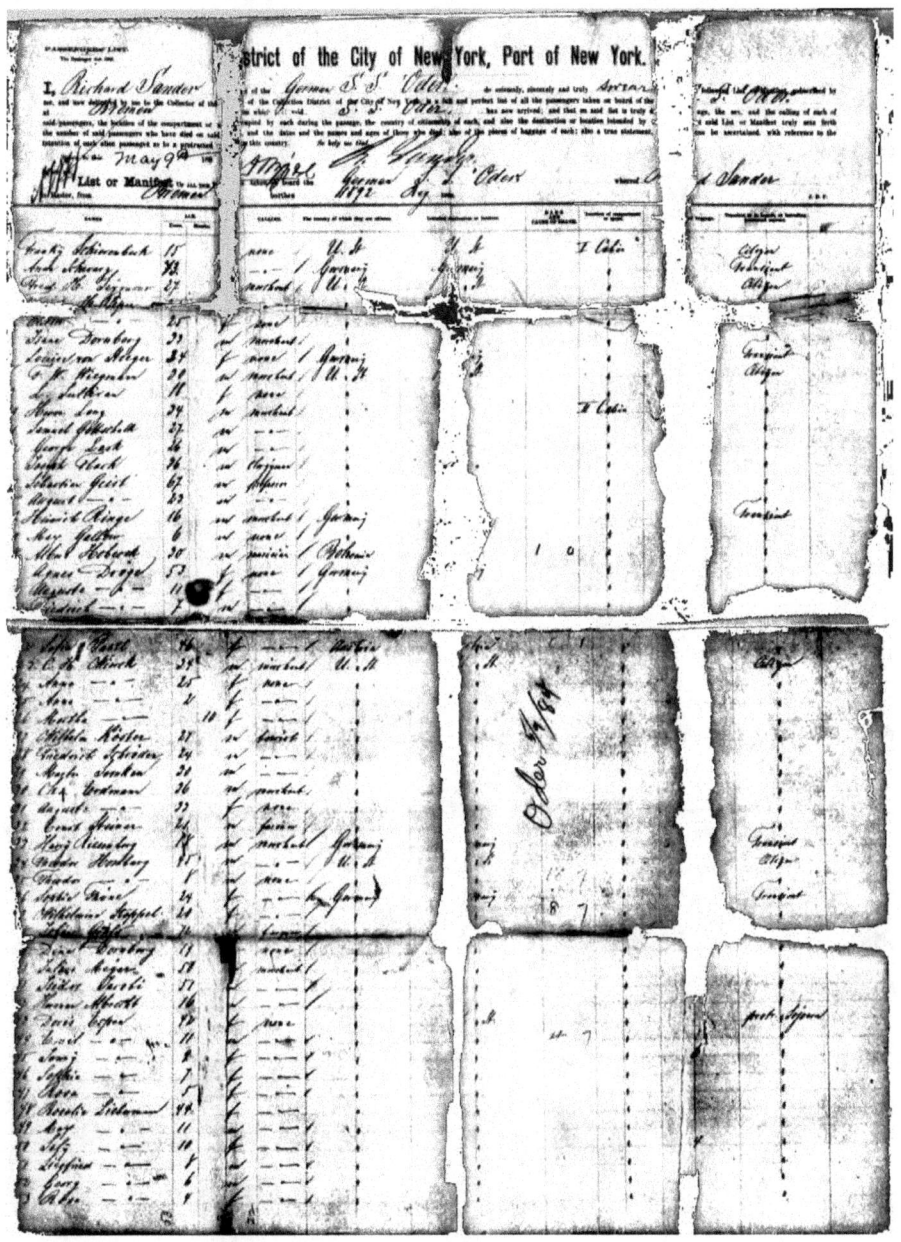

9 May 1884 Passenger Manifest for the S.S. Oder; pg 1
National Archives Series m237, Roll 476, List 517

Title Page of the Oder's Passenger Manifest

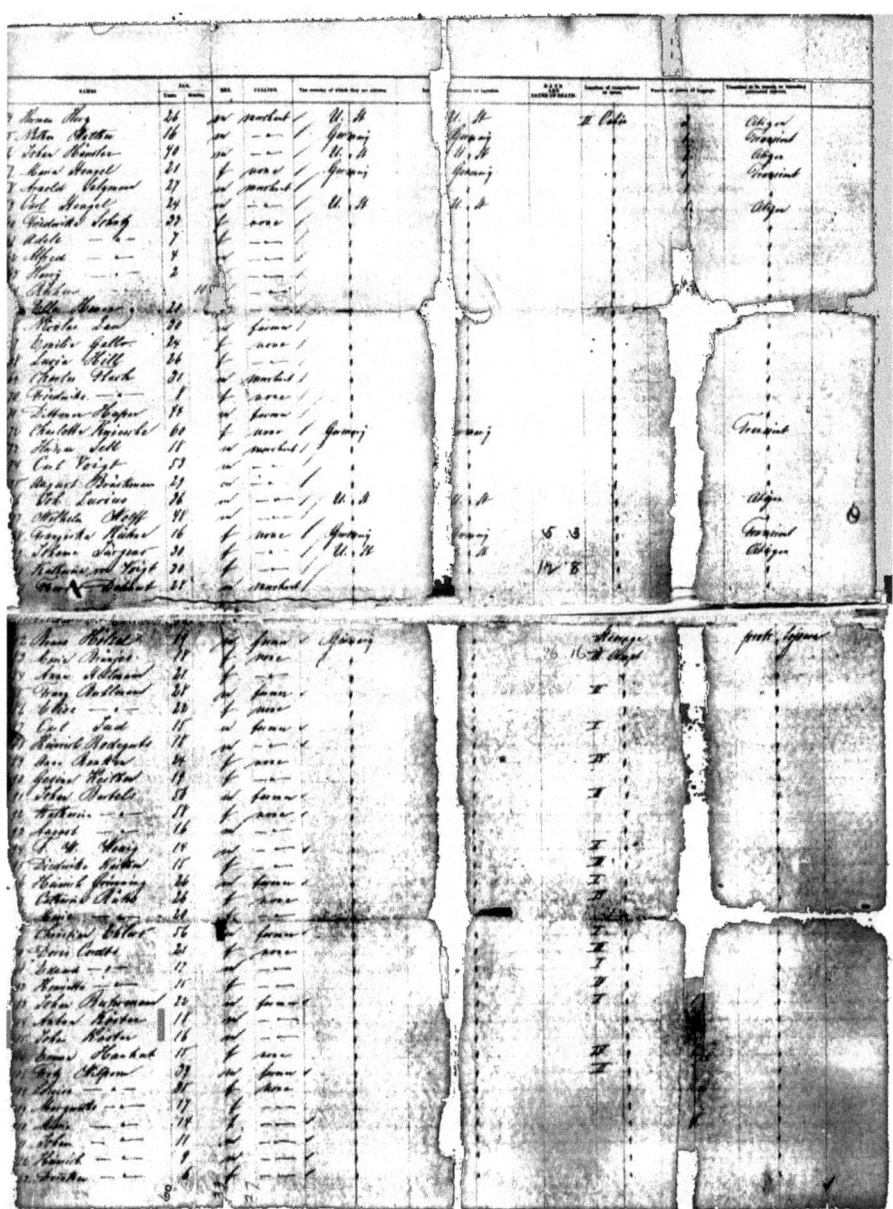

9 May 1884 Passenger Manifest for the S.S. Oder; pg 2
National Archives Series m237, Roll 476, List 517
Anton and John Koester (9th and 10th from bottom of page) arrive in the United States.

11 May 1909 Passenger Manifest for the S.S. Kronprinzessin Cecilie; left side
National Archives Series t715, Roll 1262, Page 164

Note that this portion of the manifest is for "Alien Passengers." See next page for right side.

11 May 1909 Passenger Manifest for the S.S. Kronprinzessin Cecilie; right side National Archives Series t715, Roll 1262, Page 164

See previous page for left side of this manifest sheet.

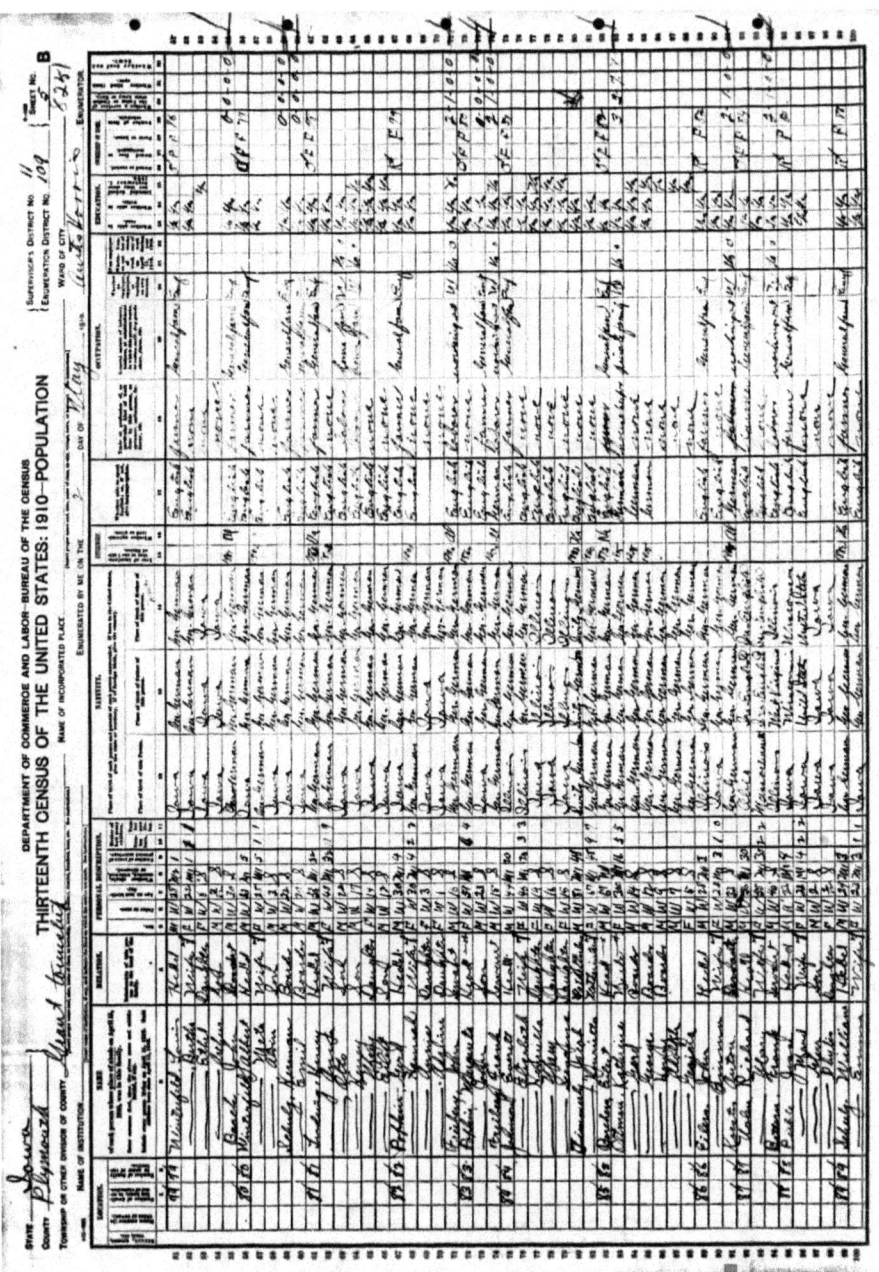

1910 U.S. Census showing Anton Koester in Grant Twp, Plymouth Cty, Ia
National Archives Series t624, Roll 418, Page 5b

*3 June 1914 Passenger Manifest for the S.S. Grosser Kurfürst; left side
National Archives Series t715, Roll , Page 8*

Anton and Katherine Bruns Koester arrive in the United States; see next page for right side.

*3 June 1914 Passenger Manifest for the S.S. Grosser Kurfürst; right side
National Archives Series t715, Roll , Page 9*

See previous page for left side of manifest sheet.

12 September 1918: World War I Draft Card for Anton Boicke Koester

29 April 1923 Passenger Manifest for the S.S. President Fillmore
National Archives Series t715, Roll 3288, Page 138

On this trip, Anton Koester appears on line 5 of the manifest for "United States Citizens"

6 August 1923 Passenger Manifest for the S.S. President Fillmore; left side National Archives Series t715, Roll 3345, Page 151, L5

Ida and her daughters appear on the "Manifest of Alien Passengers." Although Dorothea was technically a citizen already, as a child she would have had no documentation of this.

6 August 1923 Passenger Manifest for the S.S. President Fillmore; right side National Archives Series t715, Roll 3345, Page 152, L5

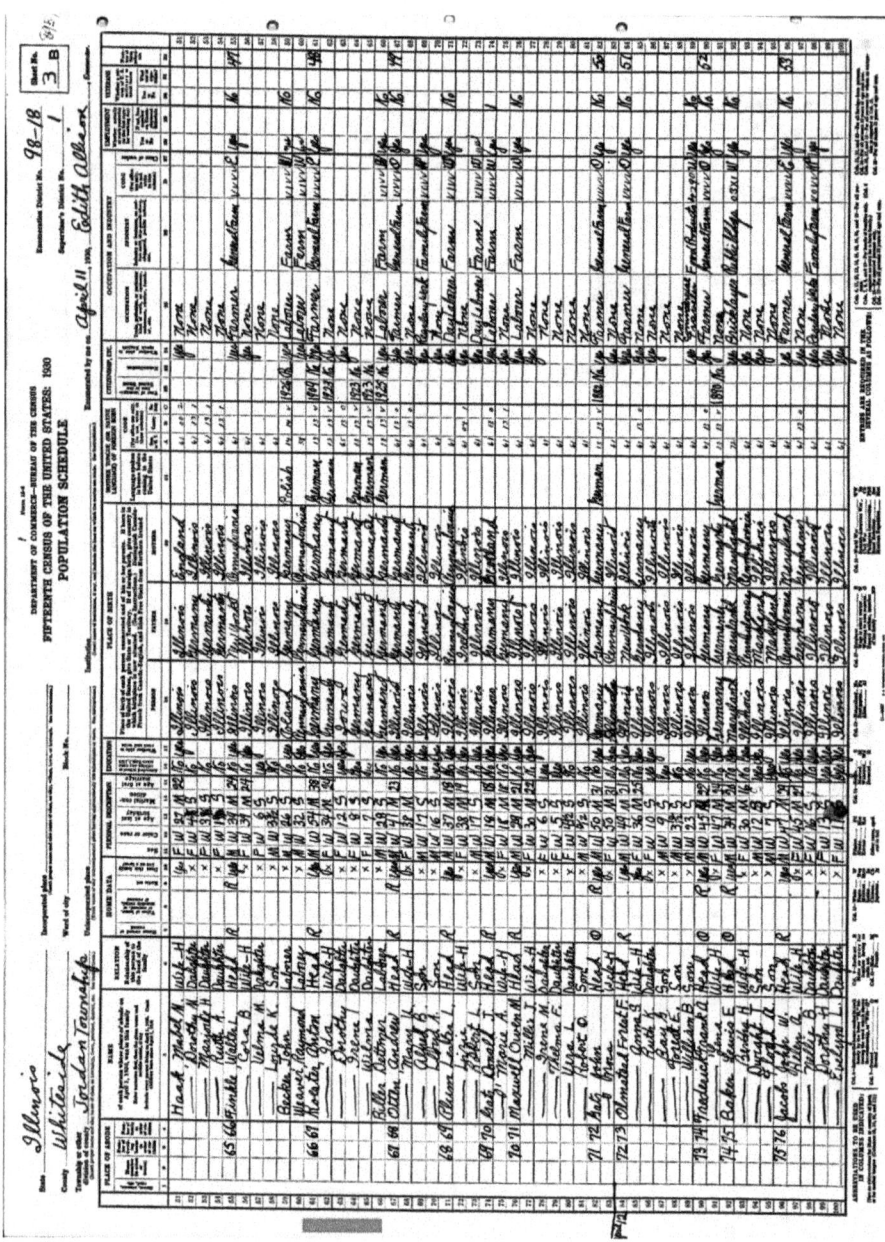

*1930 U.S.Census showing Anton Koester family in Jordan Twp, Whiteside Cty, IL
National Archives Series t626, Roll 566, Page 3b*

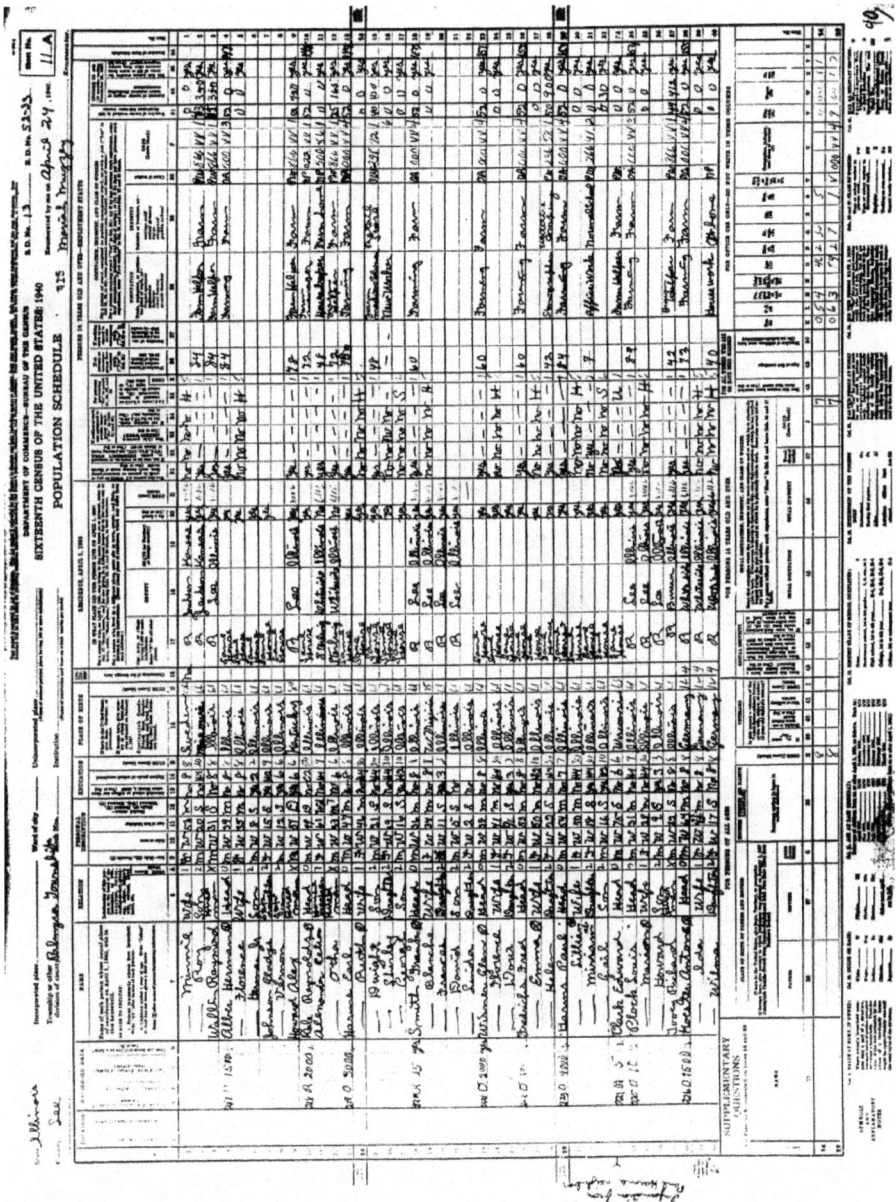

1940 U.S. Census showing Anton Koester's family in Palmyra Twp, Lee Cty, IL National Archives Series t627, Roll 836, Page 849. Sheet 11a, shows Anton, his wife Ida, and their daughter Wilma as the last three names on the page. Their last son Wesley is shown on the following page.

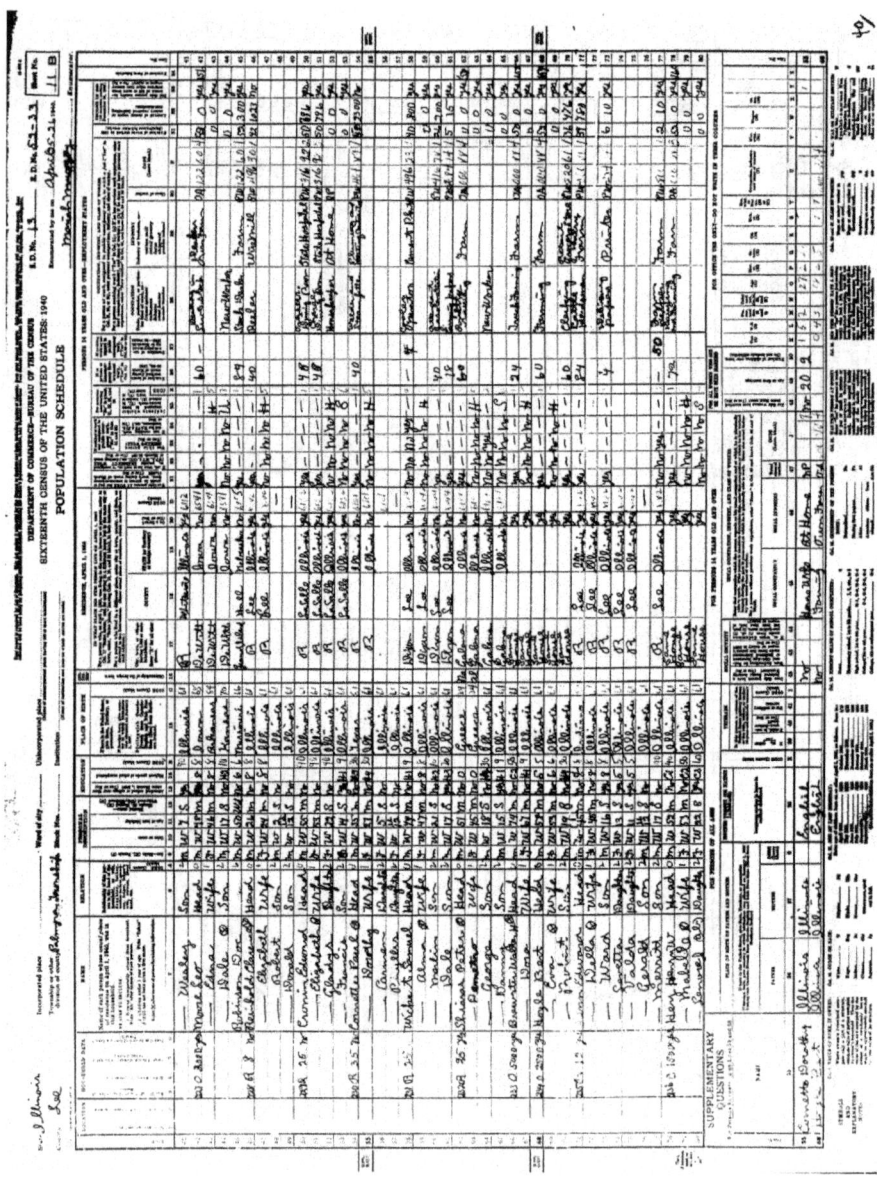

1940 U.S. Census showing Anton Koester's family in Palmyra Twp, Lee Cty, IL National Archives Series t627, Roll 836, Page 850. Sheet 11b shows Anton and Ida's youngest son Wesley at age 7; his parents and older siblings are shown on the previous page.

Wesley's Scrapbook

My grandfather was Folkert Koester born in 1845 and died in 1887, then my grandmother married Zubelt Collman in 1893. She was born in 1849 and passed away in 1934.

They had four children

Otto born 1874 and died in 1967
My Dad born 1876 and died in 1946
Anna born 1878 and died in 1900
Johann born 1883 and died in 1962.

My father was born on March 31, 1876 the son of Folkert and Marie (nee Sanders) Koester in Clevens, Germany. In 1909 he came to the United States. Five years later he returned to Germany and married Katherine Bruns on May 16, 1914. They came back to the United States the same year and took up farming around Chatsworth and Le Mars, Iowa. They were blessed with two children a son Frederick born in 1916 and a daughter Dorothea Marie Katherine born Sept. 21, 1917.

A terrible flue broke out in 1918 and many people died as did my fathers wife and son. After about 1 year my father and the daughter went back to Germany and on June 20, 1920 my father married his first wife's sister Ida Annette Bruns. My two sisters Irene on May 28, 1921 and Wilma on Sept 16, 1922. were born in Germany.

Family History Notes from Wesley Koester's Scrapbook; page 1

1924 to 1928

Things got bad in Germany and Dad came back to the United States in the Spring of 1923. When he got enough money saved he sent for my mother and three sisters. They arrived at Ellis Island on the 2nd of Aug. 1923 but were unable to land as President Harding passed away that day and no one was allowed to work, so they had to stay on board ship for three days until after the funeral. There first home was in a house near Prairieville, Illinois. After living there they moved to a house in a place called Goose Hollow. It was down a lane.

They didn't have a car at that time so they went places in the horse and buggy. Shortly after that they got there first car one that had side curtains on it. My brother Werner was born while they lived there but passed away when he was seven weeks old from a stomack disorder.

They became members of the 2nd Ave. Lutheran church of Sterling. Rev William Voeltz was the Pastor.

1928 to 1932.

In the Spring of 1928 they moved to a farm close to Polo. They had a big farm and always had hired men. Aunt Sini and her husband lived with them for awhile when they came from Germany. They lived there for four years. My sister Dorothy graduated from 8th grade and was confirmed when they lived there.

Family History Notes from Wesley Koester's Scrapbook; page 5

My Grandsons' Koester-side Ahnentafel Chart

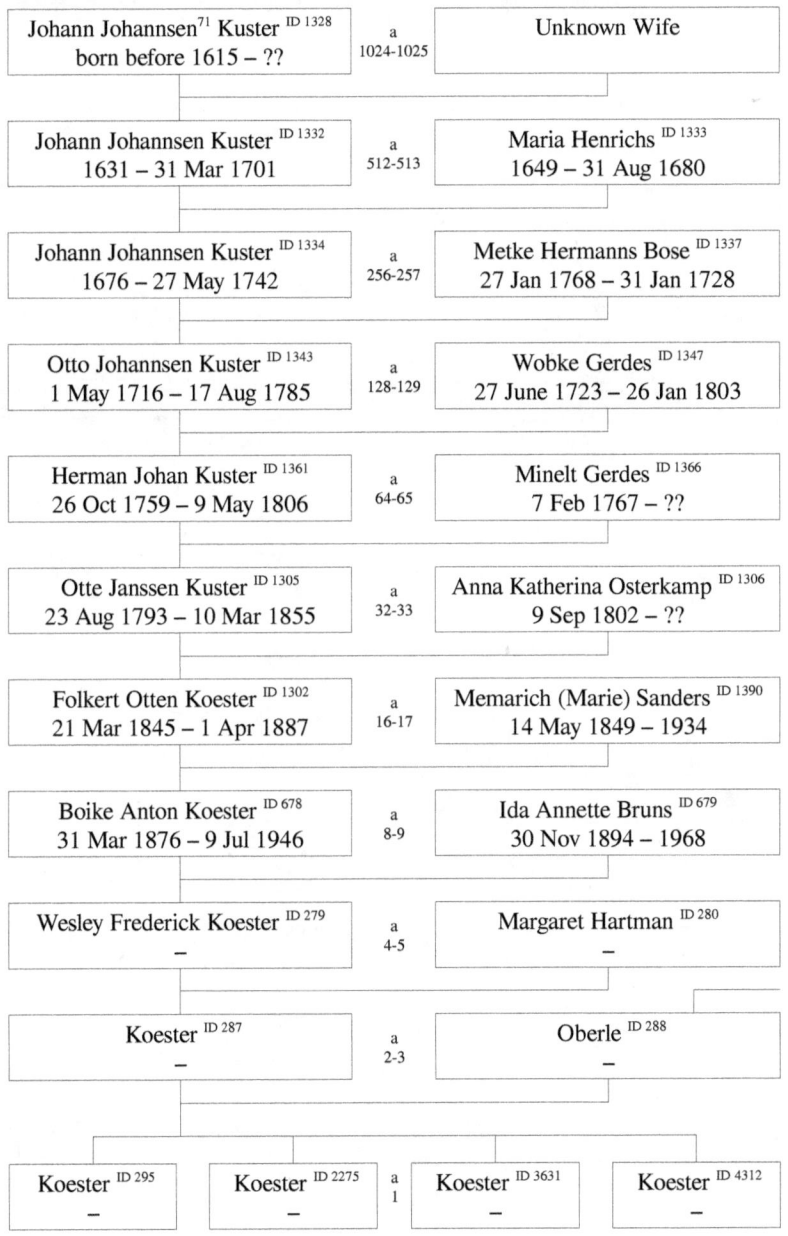

An Ahnentafel chart showing my Grandsons' Hartman-side is on page 46.

---

[71] The middle name Johannsen indicates, of course, that his father was also named Johann.

The Koster Family Album

This final section is a reproduction of *The Koster Family Album*, which began as a German language family history of the Koster family in 1928. The history of this document is given on page 1 of the booklet itself, reproduced on page 135 below, and so will not be repeated here.

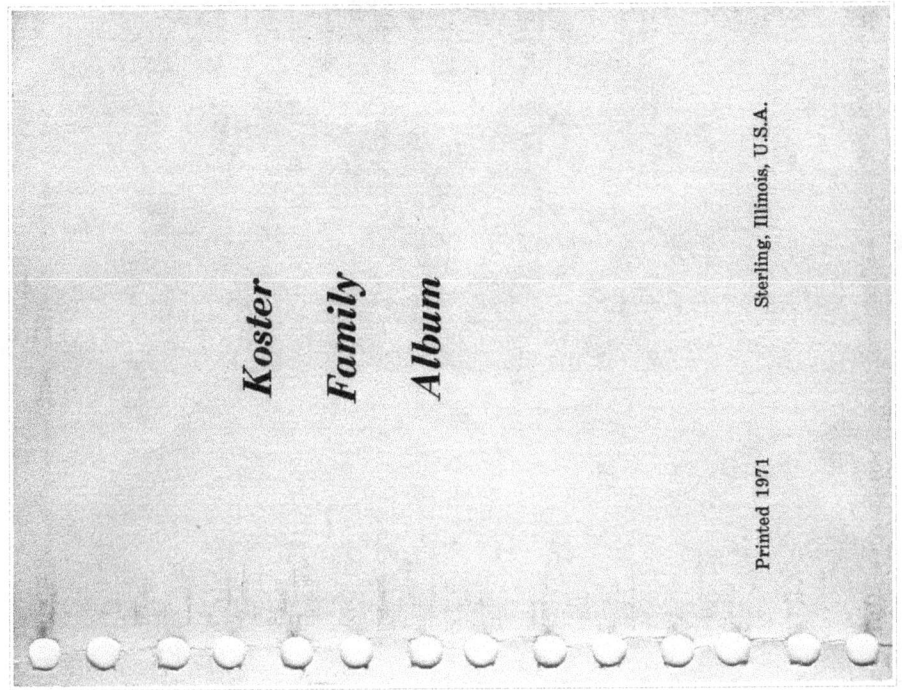

KOSTER II

The coat of arms of the Koster family and how it looks like:

Dominant colours: gold, blue, silver. On a blue ground there is a silver flail of war on a golden shaft in a right diagonal position, suited by two heads of eagles in silver. In the middle (on the top) there is a helmet with leave-shaped forms in blue-silver on both sides. On the top of whole there is a virgin-trunk in blue with a golden crown between wide opened silvery wings.

The family is Lutheran.

In Biersum and Norden in Ostfriesland, Gross Wassens, Jever, Middelswarfen, Oldenburg, Rahrdum, Rustringen, Sengwarden in Oldenburg, Havelberg in the Mark Brandenburg, Boddin in Mecklenburg (Germany), Sterling, in Illinois, Genesee, Moscow, Twin Falls in Idaho, Lakefield in Minnesota, Council Bluffs in Iowa, Emerson in Nebraska, Mount Angel in Oregon, (U.S.A.) and Cluny in Canada. (This was in 1928)

The line of Koster II, also mentioned as "Kuster" in secondhand parish registers, is well-known in Biersum, districted to Wittmund, in the middle of the 17th century. There is also to find a branch line until these days. The name of this line has always been heired as "Koster" even in all descriptions in Low German. In the registers of the Church in Biersum (1678-1727) we already can find the name "Koster" signed by Johann Johannsen Koster III, but at first in the beginning of the 19th century this way of writing the name "Koster" has been assorted successfully.

Sources of the above-mentioned you will find in the parish registers of the mentioned places and in the Church-minutes of Biersum. And in notes of the mayor a. D. Itzen of Weener, to find in the parish registers of Osteel.

Up-to-date records were assembled and published by Otto Johannes IX m. in 1928. in 1943 Ronald X d. and his mother, Marie, translated the 1928 copy from German to English.

Rose, wife of Werner IX f., traveled to U.S.A. in 1968, researched the entire family to the present time.

Rose, along with Ronald, caused this genealogy to be printed in 1971.

—1—

Symbols:
* = born
oo = married to
+ = died
d.o. = daughter of
s.o. = son of
ib = ibidem
par = parish

DIRECT LINAGE

I. Johann Johannsen Kuster (?)
   Son, *____, +____: see II

II. Johann Johannsen Kuster
    * ____, 1631; + Biersum, 3-31-1701: ____@:; oo @ 5-20-1675 to Maria Henrichs, * ____, 1649, + Biersum 8-31-1680: d.o. Henrich Eylers, of Updorf.
    Children, * at Biersum.
    1. Johann Johannsen, see III
    2. Henrich, bapt. 4-24-1678, + @ 2-24-1682.
    3. Gretke, bapt. 8-25-1680, ____; X @ 7-2-1704 to Siefke Johannsen,* ____ at Leepens, cong. Biersum.

III. Johann Johannsen Kuster (Koster)
     * Biersum 1676; buried West-Schleperhausen, parish Biersum 5-27-1742: houseman and church elder ib; X West-Schleperhausen 1-19-1702, to Metke Hermanns Bose, bapt. ib 1-27-1678; buried Biersum 1-31-1728, d.o. Hermann (Harmen) Bose *____; buried @ 2-12-1709, houseman at West-Schleperhausen, and his wife Metke *____ 1646, buried Biersum 1-31-1721.
     Children: 1-3 at Biersum, 4-7 at West-Schleperhausen:
     1. Maria, bap. 1-2-1703, +____; +____
     2. Anke bap. 9-27-1705, +____; oo @ 7-11-1732 to Eylert Johannsen, houseman.
     3. Johann Johannsen, see IV a.
     4. Metke, * 9-27-1710, buried ib 12-1-1722.
     5. Harmen, * 7-12-1713, + ib 6-18-1720.
     6. Otto Johannsen, see IV b.
     7. Gretke, bap. 7-23-1719, + ____.

IV a. Johann Johannsen Kuster.
     Bap. Biersum 3-13-1708, + ib 11-24-1743, houseman ib; oo 6-15-1734 Anna Elizabeth Gerdes, from Leerhafe, *____, +____.
     Children at Biersum:
     1. Metke Maria * 2-7-1735, +____
     2. Talke Margarethe, * 5-25-1736, +____

IV b. Otto Johannsen Kuster.
     Bap. West Schleperhausen 5-1-1716, + @ 8-17-1785; houseman ib, church and hospital board members at Biersum. oo ib 7-21-1746 to Wobke Gerdes, * Upstede, cong. Burhafe 6-27-1723, + Biersum 1-26-1803; d.o. Gerd Frerks,* ____ at Upstede and his wife Inse Folkerts, * Burhafe 10-13-1698, + Upstede 11-23-1788.
     Children at West-Schleperhausen.
     1. Johann,* 3-26-1747, + ib 4-4-1747.
     2. Johann,* 6-9-1748, + ib 6-22-1748.
     3. Gerd Otten, see V a.

-3-

I   Johann Johannsen
II Johann Johannsen 1631-1701
III Johann Johannsen 1676-1742

IV a. Johann Johannsen   IV b. Otto Johannsen
     1708-1743 no desc.   1716-1785

IV b. Otto Johannsen   V a. Gerd Otten
                             b. Frerich Otten
                             c. Herman Johann
                             d. Volgnard Otten
                                1762-1800 no desc.

V a. Gerd Otten   VI a. Tjard Oltmans
     1749-1804   1783-1807 no desc.

V b. Frerich Otten   VI b. Burchard Friedrich
     1757-1824

V c. Herman Johann   VI c. Otto Johannsen
     1759-1806

                            VI d. Otte Jansen

VI b. Burchard Friedrich   VII a. Frerich Otten 1st (Aseler) branch
      1790-1868
                            VII b. Warner Rohlfs 2nd (Zissenhauser) branch

                            VII c. Otto Johannsen 3rd (Tyedmerswafen) branch

VI c. Otto Johannsen   VII d. Johann Christean 4th (Peddewarder) branch
      1801-1882
                            VII e. Burchard Friedrich 5th (Waddewarder) branch

VI d. Otte Johannsen   VII f. Herman Theodor 6th (Biersumer) branch
      1793-1855
                            g. Folkert Otten 7th (Rahrdumer) branch

-2-

4. Johann Harms, * 1-24-1752, + Grosswarfen, cong. Eggelingen, 9-27-1822; houseman ib; oo ib 8-12-1785 to Eva Jacobs, * ___, + Middoge 12-8-1813, widow of Jurgen Eiben Kappelmanns, houseman at Grosswarfen.
5. Frerick * 12-29-1754, + West-Schleperhausen 2-8-1756.
6. Frerick Otten, see V b.
7. Hermann Johann, see V c.
8. Volquard (Folkert) Otten, see V d.
9. Melke Maria * 2-16-1765, + ib 2-24-1810; oo West-Schleperhausen 2-7-1792 to Behrend Janssen, * ___, + Blersum 12-19-1828, wharf-man ib, son of Jan Behrens, houseman at Leerhafe.

V a. Gerd Otten, * West-Schleperhausen 9-7-1749, + Itzhausen, cong. Eggelingen 8-28-1804; houseman ib; oo West-Schleperhausen 9-27-1770 to Ancke Wilken, *¹ Grashausen, cong. Wittmund 7-11-1750, + Itzhausen 9-17-1807 d.o. Wilke Janssen, houseman at Grashausen and his wife Mareyke.

Children: 1-3 at Grashausen, 4-10 at Itzhausen.
1. Otto Gerdes, * ___-1771, + Itzhausen 5-22-1790.
2. Mareken,* ___-1772, + Itzhausen 7-27-1793.
3. Wobke Maria, * ___-1776, + Itzhausen 2-11-1795.
4. Gesche, * 1-16-1778, + ___
5. Daughter born dead, 3-1-1779.
6. Johann Wilken, * 4-10-1780, + ib 2-4-1800.
7. Tjard Oltmanns, see VI a.
8. Gesche Catharina, * 9-7-1785, + ib 8-18-1787.
9. Siebelt Frerichs, * 8-16-1788, + ib 8-17-1793.
10. Gesche Catharina, * 5-2-1792, + ___

V b. Frerick Ottens Kuster, * West-Schleperhausen 1-2-1757, + Gross-Munchhausen, cong. Middoge 7-24-1824; houseman at Barums cong. Eggelingen; oo Middoge f. congr. Vittmund 5-15-1788 to Anna Catharina Borcherts; @ 1-20-1758, + ___ d.o. Borchert Friedrich Otten, * Updorf 4-16-1716, + ib 5-29-1792, heir to houseman at Updorf and Warfen; oo Warfen, cong. Eggelingen, 8-4-1740 to Anna Maria Hinrichs, * ib 7-23-1724, + Updorf 5-13-1805.

Children born at Barums:
1. Wobke Margarethe, * 7-6-1788, + @ 2-15-1859; oo twice—a.) Dunum, 10-1-1808 to Siebelt Otten * ___-1779, + Barums 5-6-1825; houseman ib. b) Eggelingen to Johann Harms Koster, * Blersum 10-6-1800, + Barums 6-28-1876; see V c. 3.
2. Burchard Friedrich, see VI b.
3. Anna Maria, * 9-22-1792, + Klein-Munchhausen, cong. Middoge, 11-24-1865; oo to Sieman Martens Schipper, * ___, + Berdumer Rieqe 9-19-1845, renter ib.
4. Metke Maria,* 1-24-1796, ___; oo Middoge 7-29-1815 to Peter Mammen Rohlfs; renter at Munchhausen, son of Warner Rohlfs, houseman at Hornum, cong. Asel, see VI c.
5. Otto Johannsen, see VI c.

V c. Herman Johann Kuster. * West-Schleperhausen 10-26-1759, + Blersum 5-9-1806; Wharfsman ib; oo West-Schleperhausen 1-6-1793 to Minelt Gerdes, * Blersum 2-7-1767, + ___; d.o. Gerd Henrichs, * Blersum 8-4-1720, + ib 4-1-1809; Wharfsman @, and his wife Ette Hinrichs * ___, +Blersum 3-14-1812.

Sons born at Blersum.
1. Otte Janssen, see VI d.
2. Gerd Hinrichs, * 5-29-1797, + ___; oo Blersum 7-12-1828 to Inse Margarethe Janssen * ___, + ___; d.o. Frerich Hinrich Janssen, houseman at Hattersum, cong. Vittmund.
3. Johann Harms, * 10-6-1800, + 6-28-1876, Barums, cong, Eggelingen; farmer ib; oo to Wobke Margarethe Koster, widow of Siebelt Otten, see V b. 1.

V d. Volquard (Folkert) Otten Kuster, * 7-23-1762, West-Schleperhausen + ___-1800; farmer at Schlushtens, cong Schortens, oo to Margarethe ___, + ___
1. ___, + ___
2. Wobke Margaretha, * ___-1797, + ___; married twice—a.) Middoge 12-30-1816 to Hero Fokken Janssen; houseman ib b) Blersum, 9-8-1840 to Berend Hinrichs Koopman, wharfsman ib.
3. Otto Janssen, * ___, + ___

VI a. Tjard Oltmanns Koster, * Itzhausen 4-12-1783, + West-Schleperhausen 11-22-1807; houseman ib; oo ib 8-2-1803 to Frauke Oncken ___-1784, + ___; d.o. Oncke Tiardes Beckman; houseman at Pockens, par. Buttforde.

Children born at West-Schleperhausen.
1. Gerd * 5-4-1804, + ___ 3-16-1814.
2. Anke Margaretha, * 1-15-1806, + ___
3. Mareken, * 11-2-1807, + ib 1-19-1809.

VI b. Burchard Friedrich Koster. * Barums 7-28-1790, + Pockens, par. Buttforde, 5-9-1868; houseman at Erichswarfen and Pockens, par. Buttforde; oo Barums, 12-30-1810 to Agnese Rohlfs, * Endzetel, par. Buttforde, 6-14-1792, + Pockens 10-24-1867, d.o. Warner Rohlfs, Buttforde 1-30-1758, + ___; houseman at Endzetel and Hornum; oo Buttforde 6-22-1791 to Insa Margaratha Peters, * Erichwarfen 1-21-1762, + ___

Children 2-9 born at Erichswarfen.
1. Insa Margaretha, * Middoge 11-21-1811, + Hofmeisterinnenburg, par. Buttforde 5-12-1863; oo Buttforde 6-12-1838 to Otte Janssen, * ___-1799, + Hofmeisterinnenburg, 2-25-1864; houseman ib; son of Johann Otten; houseman at Tjuchen, con. Leerhafe and his wife Greke ___, + ___
2. Anna Catharina, * 8.22-1813, + Bargstede, cong. Stedesdorf, 10-9-1890; oo Buttforde 7-31-1840 to Adde Siebels Adden, * ___-1793, + Endzetel 2-10-1851; houseman ib; son of Dode Olrich Adden and his wife Jabe Maria * ___, + ___

3. Wobke Maria, * 2-25-1815, + 5-27-1815.
4. Frerick Otten, see VII a. First (Aseler) branch.
5. Gretke, * 2-5-1818, + Pockens, 12-11-1862.
6. Warner Rohlfs, see VII b. Second (Zissenhauser) branch.
7. Otto Johannsen, see VII c., Third (Tyedmerswarfer) branch.
8. Wobke Maria, * 8-13-1824, + Toquard par, 4-20-1909, oo Egglingen 5-2-1851 to Folkert Janssen, * ——, + ——, Toquard 2-3-1880; houseman ib; s.o. Johann Cornelius Janssen, houseman ib and his wife Amcke Margaretha Folkerts.
9. Peter Mammen, * 3-15-1827, + Pockens 11-11-1862.

VI c. Otto Johannsen Koster. * Barums cong. Eggelingen, 11-19-1801, + Waddewarden 7-15-1882; land-lord ib; oo Middoge 8-5-1820 to Hilke Catharina Carstens *, 2-12-1797, + Warrewarden 2-8-1865, d.o. Johann Christean Carstens * ——-1760, + Middoge 12-23-1826, schoolteacher ib; and his wife Gretke Janssen * ——, + Middoge 2-25-1797.

Children, 4-6 born at Waddewarden:
1. Friedrich Otten, on visit from Munchhausen to Westerholt 9-4-1820, + Waddewarden 12-7-1839.
2. Johann Christean, see VII d. Fourth (Feddewarder) branch.
3. Anna Catharina, Munchhausen 11-7-1825, ——; oo to Claas Becker, landlord, migrated to the United States of America.
4. Burchard Friedrich, see VII e., Funfter (Waddewarder) branch.
5. Johanne Catharine Friederike, * 2-24-1834, + —— near Berlin ——; oo to Heinrich Diedrich Lubsen, landlord at Labsenburg, cong. Waddewarden.
6. Ottilie Henriette, * 4-22-1836, + Varel in Oldenburg ——; oo to Heinrich Eilers, merchant at Varelerhafen.

VI d. Otte Janssen Koster. * Blersum 8-23-1793, + ib 3-10-1855; wharfsman ib; oo ib 4-23-1825 to Anna Catharina Osterkamp, * Westerburg 9-9-1802, + Blersum 3-9-1892, d.o. Folkert Hinrichs Osterkamp, tax-collector at Westerburg, and his wife Rienelt Hicken.

Children born at Blersum:
1. Minelt, * 8-14-1825, + ib 5-1-1826.
2. Minelt Maria, * 5-14-1831, + Oldenburg ——; oo Blersum 5-14-1855 to Harm Janssen, ib, + Asel 12-30-1828, killed by falling oak 12-13-1858; contractor ib.
3. Rienelt Margaretha, * 12-14-1834, + Wilhelmshaven 2-28-1899; oo to Ihnke Eimen, Rahrdum, + Jever.
4. Hermann Theodor, see VII f., Sixth (Biersumer) branch.
5. Folkert Otten, see VII g., Seventh (Rahrdumer) branch.

— 6 —

FIRST (ASELER) BRANCH (Extinct)

VII a. Frerich Otten Koster. * Erichswarfen 4-30-1816, + Asel 8-28-1890; landlord ib; oo to Trientke Maria Bennen, * Asel 4-4-1825, + ib 10-31-1907.

Children born at Minsen:
1. Agnes * 1825; + Asel 9-6-1924. oo to Heinrich Bennen, landlord ib.
2. Johann Friedrich, * 1865, + ib. 1871.
3. Anton Georg, see VIII a.

VIII a. Anton Georg Koster. * Minsen 10-19-1869, + Wittmund, 1918; mill owner at Asel; oo to Amalie Catherine Schonbohm, * Fahnhusen, cong. Blersum, 2-10-1873, + Wittmund 3-5-1921.

Children born at Asel:
1. Maria Wilhelmine, * 1-30-1895; oo Wittmund, 6-30-1921 to Johann Bohlken, tax secretary at Aurich.
2. Meta Catharine, * 2-8-1897; oo Wittmund to Gerhard Badberg, principal at Wilhelfsfehn near Grossefehn.
3. Fritz Otto, * 10-9-1899, + ib 2-18-1900.
4. Annchen Elise, * 8-20-1904.
5. Agnes Ottilie Johanne, * 6-21-1907.

SECOND (ZISSENHAUSER) BRANCH

VII b. Warner Rohlfs   1820-1906

VIII a. Buchard Friedrich
VIII b. Hero
VIII d. Peter Mammen
VIII e. Frerich Otten
VIII f. Heinrich Theodor
   1. Werner—1900
   2. Herbert—1905

VIII b. Buchard Fredrich   1856-1926

VIII d. Peter Mammen   1872-
   1. Rudolph—1902

VIII e. Frerich Otten   1874-
   1. Walter—1910

VIII f. Heinrich Theodor
   1. Adolph—1912
   2. Werner—1914
   3. Otto—1922

— 7 —

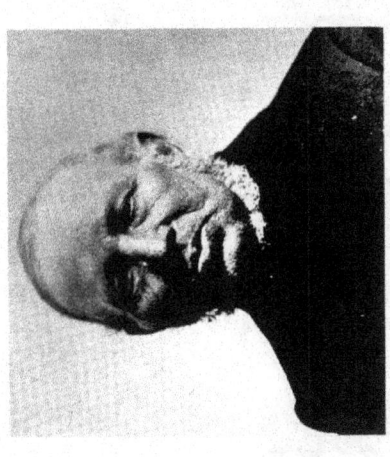

VII b—Warner Rohlfs

SECOND (ZISSENHAUSER) BRANCH

VII b. Warner Rohlfs Koster. * Erischwarfen 3-15-1820, + Middoge 6-3-1906; landlord at Zissenhauser near Tettens; oo Buttforde 3-1-1856 to Helene Christine Redelfs, * Blersum 3-9-1836, + Middoge 12-20-1892; d.o. Hero Redelfs, * Blersum 2-21-1802, + ib 5-24-1849, and his wife Elizabeth Eden.

Children 1-3 born at Blersum, 4-8 at Kaperei, cong. Hohenkirchen.
1. Burchard Friedrich, see VIII b.
2. Agnese Hermine, * 2-13-1859; oo Tettens 12-31-1883 to Hero (Herman) Tjarks Koster, * Klen-Warfen 3-25-1857; + Sterling, Ill. U.S.A. 1-18-1901; farmer ib; see VIII h.
3. Hero, see VIII c.
4. Elise, * 1-22-1867; oo Tettens 10-28-1896 to Johann Ahrends, * Werdumer-Altendeich 2-11-1861, landlord at Zissenhausen, son of Mamme Ahrends and his wife Insine Theodore Johanne Janssen.
5. Insine Margarethe, * 12-20-1869; oo 5-3-1893 to Johann Abels, * Sillenstede 7-6-1857, + ib. 5-15-1918; landlord ib.
6. Peter Mammen, see VIII d.
7. Frerich Otten, see VIII e.
8. Henrich Theodor, see VIII f.

— 8 —

VIII b. Burchard Friedrich Koster. * Blersum 5-30-1856, + Rittershausen cong. St. Joost, 12-10-1926; landlord ib; oo Hohenkirchen 10-27-1898 to Helene Martens, * Cleverns, 8-6-1870.
Children born at Wiarder-Altendeich
1. Werner, * 8-21-1900.
2. Helene Catharine, * 3-27-1902; oo 2-1-1923 to Johann Heinrich Abel, * Neerstedt 4-19-1885, businessman at Bretdorf, son of Arend Abel * Neerstedt 2-2-1852; + ib. 12-20-1918; builder ib; oo 7-31-1882 to Adeline Rudebusch, * Geveshausen 5-3-1859, + Neerstedt 1-29-1914.
3. Herbert, * 10-26-1905.

VIII c. Hero Koster. * Blersum 5-13-1863; landlord at Sengwarden; oo 11-4-1891 to Ida Adeline Ihnken, * ib 4-22-1858, + 8-20-1928, d.o. Ihnke Hajen Ihnken, * ib 3-7-1817, +——, and his first wife Eva Gehardine Gerrits, * Tammhausen 10-29-1831, +——, Sengwarden.
Daughter born at Utters, cong. Sengwarden:
1. Helene, * 7-27-1892.

VIII c—Hero and Ida

— 9 —

VIII d—Peter and Mary

VIII d. Peter Mammen Koster, * Kaperei 1-16-1872, farmer at Mount Angel, Oregon; oo Melvin, Iowa 1-11-1900 to Mary Liehr, * Niederohman, County Hersfeld, 11-19-1874. Children 1-4 born at Ashton in Iowa:
1. Alma Katharine * 10-21-1900; oo Mount Angel, Oregon, 11-25-1920 to Richard Medack, * Los Angeles, Calif. 5-26-1896, farmer at Mount Angel.
2. Rudolph Johannes, * 10-10-1902.
3. Fritz Warner, * 4-29-1904, + Mount Angel 9-24-1925.
4. Helene Mary, * 7-19-1911.
5. Irene Leona, * Mount Angel 4-15-1918.

—10—

VIII e—Frerich and Gesine

VIII e. Frerich Otten Koster, * Kaperei 9-15-1874; landlord at Middelswarfen, Jeverland; oo 11-18-1907 to Gesine Drantmann, * Tettens 2-3-1875, d.o. Johann Mienits Drantmann, * Hamshausen near Tettens 8-20-1835, + Tettens 7-11-1908 and his wife Mareken Gesine Drantmann, * Schleperhausen near Jever 12-31-1838, + Tettens 5-19-1902. Son born at Hohensminde, par., Wiarden:
1. Walter Johannes, * 12-16-1910.

—11—

VIII f.—Heinrich

VIII f. Henrich Theodor Koster, * Kaperei 12-27-1876, buyer at Oldenburg; oo Leer 5-14-1911 to Minna Onkes, * 4-4-1884. Children 2-4 born at Oldenburg:
1. Adolph Werner, * Leer 4-14-1912.
2. Werner Heinrich, * 12-6-1914.
3. Lotte Mathilde, * 12-30-1919.
4. Otto Conrad, * 1-17-1922.

—12—

THIRD (TYEDMERSWARFER) BRANCH
Eighth Generation

VII c. Otto Johannsen
1822-1917

VIII g. Burchard Fredrich, no desc.
h. Hero (Herman) Tjarks
i. Frerich Otten (Otto)
k. Hajo Theodor
l. Johann Peter
m. Warner Rohlfs
n. Nicolaus Friedrich Peter

Ninth Generation

VIII h. Hero (Herman) Tjark
1857-1901

IX a. Rudolph Warner
b. Herbert Arthur
c. Theodore Alfred
d. Friedrich Herman

VIII i. Frerich Otten (Otto)
1860-1903

IX e. Otto Johannes
f. Werner Rudolph

VIII k. Hajo Theodore
1863-1942

IX g. Otto Theodore
h. Heinrich Fredrick
i. Arthur Herman
j. Albert Edward

VIII l. Johann Peter
1870-1939

IX k. Otto Janssen
l. Albert Paul

VIII m. Warner Rohlfs
1873-1941

IX m. Otto Johannes
n. Jacob Warner
o. Werner Rohlf Burchard

VIII n. Nicolaus Friedrich Peter
1876-1952

IX 1. Otto Ihno—1912-1942
2. Ihno Luppo Burchard—1913-1944
3. Siegfried Hajo Theodor—1916-1941
4. Warner Rohlf Peter—1917-1936

—13—

Tenth Generation

IX a. Rudolph Warner
       1887-
    X a. Carl Herman
       b. Walter Fredrick
       c. Elmer Louis
       d. Ronald William

IX b. Herbert Arthur
       1889-1971
    X e. Arthur Henry

IX c. Theodore Alfred
       1892-
    X f. Russell Wesley
       g. Merrill Theodore
       h. Wesley Herman

IX d. Friedrich Herman
       1896-1959
    X i. Edwin Edward
       j. Lawrence Jacob

IX e. Otto Johannes
       1889-1936
    X k. Burchard Frerich Otten

IX f. Werner Rudolph
       1902-1945
    X l. Hajo

IX g. Otto Theodore
       1891-1970
    X m. Raymond Theodore

IX h. Heinrich Friedrich
       1895-
    X n. Ralph Eugene

IX i. Arthur Herman
       1901-
    X o. John Earl

IX j. Albert Edward
       1907-
    X p. Richard Arthur

IX k. Otto Janssen
       1893-
    X q. Roland Alexander

IX l. Albert Paul
       1900-
    X r. Paul Raymond

IX m. Otto Johannes
       1901-1969
    X s. Burchard Otto Werner
       t. Hajo Wilhelm
       u. Otto Heinrich

IX n. Jacob Werner
       1902-1960
    Daughters

IX o. Werner Rohlf Burchard
       1923-
    X v. John Henry

Eleventh Generation

X a. Carl Herman
     1917-
    XI a. John Carl
        Carl Henry XII

X q. Roland Alexander
     1919-
    XI b. Bruce Alexander
        Brian Bruce XII

THIRD (TYEDMERSWARFER) BRANCH

VII c. Otto Johannsen Koster. * Erichswarfen April 17, 1822, + Tettens March 31, 1917, farmer in Tyedmerswarfen, oo Asel April 24, 1854 to Maria Tjarks, * Hornum par. Asel July 12, 1831, + Kleinengroden par. Middoge June 11, 1920, d.o. Hero Tjarks, * House Berdum October 22, 1798, + Asel March 16, 1856, owner of a house and innkeeper ib., oo Hornum par. Asel June 16, 1825 to Tjatke Margarethe Oncken, * Klinge par. Asel October 6, 1802, + Hornum May 9, 1835. Children: 1-3 born in Kleinwarfen par. Eggelingen, 4-10 in Tyermerswarfen.

1. Burchard Friedrich, see VIII g.
2. Hero (Hermann) Tjarks, see VIII h.
3. Frerich Otten (Otto), see VIII i.
4. Hajo Theodor, see VIII k.
5. Agnese (Agnes) Margarethe, * December 31, 1863, + Kleinengroden March 13, 1953, oo Tettens April 30, 1890 to Heinrich Friedrich Graaffs, * Carolinengroden December 1, 1850, domainlandholder, + Kleinengroden January 25, 1930.
6. Tjatke Elise Marie, * July 14, 1866, + Sandhorst near Aurich December 26, 1916.
7. Insine Katharine, * March 1, 1868, + Brake on Weser August 26, 1951, oo Tettens September 10, 1898 to Hinrich Heeren Hinrichs, * Berdum April 21, 1875, miller in Nesse, + Brake on Weser May 24, 1958.
8. Johann Peter, see VIII l.
9. Warner Rohlfs, see VIII m.
10. Nicolaus Friedrich Peter, see VIII n.

VII c—Otto and Maria

VIII g—Marie, Burchard, Agnes, Annchen, Marie

VIII g. Burchard Friedrich Koster, * Kleinwarfen March 21, 1855, +
Jever June 25, 1927, farmer in Carlseck/Hohenkirchen, a) oo Pockens par. Buttforde May 7, 1884 to Hieske Marie Beckmann, * Pockens April 24, 1856, + Carlseck January 4, 1887. b) oo Minsen October 8, 1890 to Marie Evers, * Hohenhenne par. Minsen November 11, 1866, + Friederikensiel July 16, 1939, d.o. Jakob Evers, * Neundorf January 23, 1839, + Hohenhenne May 2, 1914, farmer, oo Wittmund April 8, 1865 to Anke Marie Beckmann, * Grasshausen April 9, 1843, + Hohenhenne April 12, 1880

Children, second marriage, born in Carlseck:
1. Annchen Marie, * July 4, 1891, + Jever March 15, 1937.
2. Marie, * May 26, 1893, + Gross-Eilshausen September 9, 1949, oo Carlseck May 2, 1914 to Reinhard, Siebels Janssen, * Friedrichsgroden November 13, 1876, + Gross-Eilshausen July 28, 1954, farmer in Gross-Eilshausen.
3. Frieda Ottilie Jacobine, * December 26, 1898, + Carlseck February 14, 1899.
4. Agnes Margaretha, * February 16, 1900, oo Carlseck May 12, 1920 to Emil Heinrich Janssen, * Friederikensiel June 26, 1891, +ib. February 18, 1953, farmer ib.

VIII h. Hero (Hermann) Tjarks Kuster-Koster, * Kleinwarfen March 25, 1857, + Sterling January 18, 1901, farmer ib., oo Tettens December 31, 1883 to Agnese Hermine Koster (female cousin "Zissenhauser" section, * Blersum February 13, 1859, + Sterling June 19, 1929, d.o. Warner Rohlfs Koster, * Erichswarfen March 15, 1820, + Middoge June 3, 1906, farmer in Zissenhausen near Tettens, oo Buttforde March 1, 1856 to Helene Christine Redelfs, * Blersum March 9, 1836, + Middoge December 1892.

Children: 1-7 in Minonk, Illinois, 8 born in Sterling, Illinois.
1. Helene Christine, * December 24, 1884, + Sterling July 9, 1957, oo Sterling June 4, 1932 to August H. Meins, * Schortens, Friesland December 14, 1876, + Sterling, Ill. September 22, 1964, farmer ib.
2. Otto Johann, * March 6, 1886, + February 4, 1966, gardener
3. Rudolph Warner, see IX a.
4. Herbert Arthur, see IX b.
5. Theodore Alfred, see IX c.
6. Friedrich, * December 18, 1893, + Minonk January 22, 1894.
7. Friedrich Herman, see IX d.
8. Wilhelm Peter, * Sterling September 2, 1898, + Sterling March 11, 1900.

VIII h—Hero (Herman), Agnese, Otto, Helene, Rudolph

VIII i. Frerich Otten (Otto), * February 22, 1860, + Ostenburg near Oldenburg October 9, 1903, pastor ib., oo Hagermarsch district Norden December 12, 1888 to Catharine Regine Foline Marie de Vries, * Deich and Sielrott October 4, 1863, + Norden September 27, 1932, d.o. Jan Claassen de Vries, farmer in Theener, * Theener January 23, 1838, + ib. January 20, 1904, oo Hilgenriedersiel May 13, 1860 to Mareka Cornelia Poppinga * Hilgenriedersiel April 26, 1833, + Theener April 27, 1894.

Children, 1-2 born in Neuenkirchen/Oldenburg, 4-7 in Ostenburg:

1. Otto Johannes, see IX e.
2. Hans Klaus, * October 21, 1891, + on sea February 7, 1914.
3. Martha Cornelia, * Oldorf November 18, 1893, + Theener February 23, 1958, oo Norden May 4, 1922 to Schweero de Vries, * Theener January 6, 1894, farmer in Theener (retired).
4. Burchard Friedrich, * February 2, 1896, + (killed) in Perthes, France February 16, 1915.
5. Erich Karl Johann, * April 4, 1898, + (killed) Middelkerke (Flandern) August 19, 1917.
6. Maria Catharina, * July 10, 1899, oo Norden September 8, 1923 to Johann Friedrich Heuer, tax expert, * Norden July 1, 1894, + ib. December 23, 1963, Maria Osnabrueck, December 25, 1969.
7. Werner Rudolph, see IX f.

VIII i.—Frerich and Catharine

VIII k. Hajo Theodor Kuster (Koster), * Tyedmerswarfen March 15, 1862, farmer in Moscow, Idaho, + Moscow January 11, 1942, oo Minonk, Ill. December 20, 1889 to Maria Janssen, * Minonk October 2, 1867, + Moscow, Idaho September 23, 1947, d.o. Henrich Folkert Janssen, oo to Trienke Harms,° 1829, + Sterling 1909. Children, 1-2 born in Minonk, 4-6 born in Rock Falls, Ill:

1. Otto Theodore, see IX g.
2. Heinrich Friedrich, see IX h.
3. Raymond Arthur, * Sterling, Ill. August 24, 1899, + Genesee, Idaho December 15, 1918.
4. Arthur Hermann, see IX i.
5. Clara Theresa Marie, * October 30, 1905, B.S. Idaho University, elementary teacher, oo Moscow, Idaho March 31, 1940 to Ezra Carid Fish, * Rollin, Texas April 30, 1902, salesman insurance.
6. Albert Edward, see IX i.

VIII k—Hajo and Marie

VIII—Johann and Brechtje

VIII 1. Johann Peter Koster, * Tyedmerswarfen November 11, 1870, farmer zu Lakefield, Minnesota, + Lakefield, Minnesota November 15, 1939, oo a) Flanagan, Illinois March 15, 1893 to Brechtje Post, * Flanagan November 2, 1872, + Lakefield, Minnesota August 20, 1917, d.o. Albert Janssen Post, farmer, * Ochtelbur, Ostfriesland June 17, 1843, landet ib U.S.A. May 20, 1867, + Flanagan, Ill. January 13, 1926, oo Riepe May 20, 1865 to Antje Nannen Ohling, * Riepe, Ostfriesland October 21, 1841, + Flanagan, Ill. April 8, 1912. b) Lakefield, Minn. October 17, 1893 to Hulda Rost, widowed, Milbrath, * March 30, 1876, Jackson County, Minn., Rost Township, + Lakefield November 30, 1956.
Children (first marriage), 1 born in Flanagan, 2-3 born in Lakefield, 4-8 born in Heron Lake, Minn.
1. Otto Janssen, see IX k.
2. Antje Dorothea, * Rost Twp., Jackson County August 25, 1895, + Lakefield July 25, 1953, oo Heron Lake August 11, 1918 to George Reinhold Milbrath, * Lakefield March 27, 1888, farmer in Rost Twp., Minn.
3. Marie Agnes, * July 2, 1898, oo Heron Lake Jan. 4, 1922 to Gustav Adolph Glasser, * Minier, Ill. Sept. 29, 1897, farmer in Heron Lake, + Dundee, Ill. Feb. 25, 1965.
4. Albert Paul, see IX l.
5. Pauline Hermine, * June 5, 1903, oo Lakefield Dec. 13, 1925 to John Conrad Albers, * Lakefield Dec. 29, 1900, farmer (retired).
6. Insine Cathrine, * July 17, 1904, Heron Lake July 31, 1904.
7. Frieda Ella Louise, * July 15, 1905, oo Rock Falls, Ill. Oct. 7, 1924 to Hermann Wessels, * Sterling, Ill. May 31, 1898, farmer, + Sterling Nov. 10, 1961.
8. Brechtje Helene Bertha, * Aug. 20, 1917, oo Lakefield Sept. 5, 1937 to Alvin Rademacher, * Lakefield Aug. 25, 1914. carpenter,

VIII m. Warner Rohlfs Koster, * Tyedmerswarfen April 18, 1873, farmer in Pommern, + Wiermar/Thuringen Sept. 2, 1941, oo a) Roffhausen April 27, 1900 to Emma Groenewold, * Roffhausen par. Sande March 16, 1873, + Wittenberge Aug. 16, 1916, d.o. Jacob Wessels Groenewold, * Sloot, Parochie Pilsum Sept. 4, 1931, + Roffhausen Jan. 22, 1910, oo a) Visquard March 20, 1861 to Barber Emen Museler * Suurhusen May 3, 1829, + Roffhausen May 8, 1882, oo b) Janken Wilken born Adden _____ oo b) Goldbeck near Wittstock/Dosse April 23, 1920 to Regine Margarethe Koschlig, * Langenbruck/Oberschlesien Jan. 30, 1890, d.o. Johannes Koschlig, miller, * Meleschwitz par. Breslau/Oberschlesien May 16, 1841, + Namslau/Schlesien _____ 1905, oo Melechwitz June 25, 1872 to Anna Paschke * Meleschwitz par. Breslau April 21, 1854, + Breslau _____ 1907.

Children, 1-6 (first marriage) born in Tyedmerswarfen, 7 (second marriage) born in Goldbeck.

1. Otto Johannes, see IX m.
2. Jacob Werner, see IX n.
3. Fritz Burchard, * May 18, 1905, + Tyedmerswarfen July 7, 1908.
4. Maria Barbara, * Oct. 15, 1908, oo Boddin/Mecklenburg Sept. 23, 1930 to Friedrich Meyer, * Brilon/Westphalen Dec. 18, 1899.
5. a Werner Rohlf, * July 10, 1912, + Tettens June 11, 1914.
   b Erich, * July 10, 1912, + Tettens May 22, 1914
7. Werner Rohlf Burchard, see IX o.

VIII m—Warner Rohlfs Koster and Regina

VIII n—Otto, Siegfried, Gretchen, Warner, Ihno

VIII n. Nicolaus Friedrich Peter Koster, * Tyedmerswarfen Oct. 4, 1876, farmer in Havelberg/Mark, + Damhusen Jan. 7, 1952, oo Kloster Sielmonken par. Emden March 10, 1911 to Gesina Ihna Ellerbroek, * Kloster Dykhusen March 3, 1885, + Emden Feb. 10, 1962, d.o. Ihno Luppen Ellerbrock, * Kloster Sielmonken Aug. 30, 1854, farmer, + Damhusen June 6, 1941, oo Rysum May 13, 1882 to Amkelina Jacobina Wiltfang, * Rysum Jan. 24, 1854, + Westerhusen Nov. 21, 1932. Children: 2-5 born in Joachimshof near Breddin, Mark Brandenburg.
1. Otto Ihno, * Gerdshagen Feb. 20, 1912, + (killed) Russland Jan. 17, 1942, artillerist.
2. Amkelina Gretchen, * July 25, 1913, + Havelberg/Mark March 12, 1944, oo Uttum July 25, 1942 to Abbo Georg Wilhelm Georgs, *Damhusen July 24, 1909, farmer in Nessmerpolder.
3. Ihno Luppo Burchard Friedrich, * Feb. 22, 1915, + (killed) March 17, 1942, Hauptmann and Staffelkapitan (captain).
4. Siegfried Hajo Theodor, * March 15, 1916, + (killed) Russland July 9, 1941, Wachtmeister (artill.)
5. Warner Rolf Peter, * May 3, 1917, + Leer, Ostfriesland July 3, 1936.
no Koster descendants

VII n—Nicolaus Peter Koster and Gesine

IX a—Rudolph and Marie

IX a. Rudolph Warner, * Dec. 8, 1887, farmer in Sterling (retired), oo Sterling Oct. 4, 1916 to Marie Morgenstern, * Sterling Oct. 21, 1898, d.o. Karl Morgenstern, * Wiebelskirchen Saar-Rheinprovinz Jan. 6, 1859, butcher, + Sterling Jan. 2, 1919 (perished), oo Rock Falls April 10, 1890 to Anna Margrete Abels, * Horumersiel, Oldenberg March 10, 1865, + Sterling April 9, 1941.
Children: 1-4 born in Sterling, Illinois.
1. Carl Hermann, see X a.
2. Walter Fredrick, see X b.
3. Elmer Louis, see X c.
4. Ronald William, see X d.

—32—

IX b—Frieda, Helen, Arthur, Herbert

IX b. Herbert Arthur, * Dec. 28, 1889, farmer (retired), + Sterling Feb. 27, 1971, oo a) Sterling Feb. 25, 1920 to Anna Wessels, * Sterling Aug. 24, 1893, + Sterling April 4, 1930, d.o. Heinrich Wessels, * Wiarden, Oldenburg Sept. 28, 1854, farmer, + Sterling April 20, 1932, oo Jordan Twp. Oldenburg Feb. 25, 1884 to Maria Henrietta Meents, * Middoge, Oldenburg April 13, 1864, + Sterling Sept. 11, 1927, oo b) Sterling Sept. 15, 1934 to Frieda Haberer, * Rotenberg/Wurttemberg July 2, 1908, d.o. Jakob Haberer, * Rotenberg/Wurttemberg May 22, 1870, businessman, + Rotenberg Feb. 22, 1915, oo Rotenberg to Anna Schuhmacher, * Rotenberg May 24, 1880, + Rotenberg Oct. 24, 1912.
Children: (first marriage) 1-2 born in Sterling.
1. Arthur Henry, see X e.
2. Helen Marie, * Jan. 24, 1923, oo Sterling Dec. 28, 1956 to William Franklin Von Holten, farmer in Lyndon, Ill., * Rock Falls, Ill. Nov. 16, 1921, s.o. Carl Lidwig Von Holten, * Sidney, Ill. Jan. 26, 1893, farmer (retired), oo Rock Falls, Ill. Dec. 20, 1919 to Beulah Williford, * Oak Grove, Tennessee Dec. 13, 1899.
3. Donald Paul, * April 3, 1930, + April 4, 1930.

—33—

IX c—Russell, Wesley, Martha, Merrill, Theodore

IX c. Theodore Alfred, * March 8, 1892, farmer (retired), oo Rock Falls, Ill. Sept. 7, 1924 to Martha Wessels, * Sterling, Ill. May 9, 1896, d.o. Heinrich Wessels, farmer, Wiarden, Oldenburg Sept. 28, 1854, + Sterling April 20, 1932, oo Jordan Twp. Feb. 25, 1884 to Maria Henrietta Meents, * Middoge, Oldenburg April 13, 1864, + Sterling Sept. 11, 1927.
Children: 1-3 born in Sterling.
1. Russell Wesley, see X f.
2. Merrill Theodore, see X g.
3. Wesley Herman, see X h.

IX d—Friedrich and Martha

IX d. Friedrich Hermann, * Dec. 27, 1896, farmer in Sterling, + Sterling Feb. 19, 1959, oo Sterling Jan. 29, 1925 to Martha Bruns, * Hartsburg, Ill. May 12, 1904, teacher (retired), d.o. Jacob Bruns, * Twixlum, Ostfriesland Oct. 4, 1875, + Rock Falls July 3, 1945, oo Hartsburg, Ill. Nov. 30, 1900 to Katie Klockenga, * Emden, Ill. Nov. 1, 1879, + Sterling Jan. 29, 1943.
Children: 1-2 born in Sterling.
1. Edwin Edward, see X i.
2. Lawrence Jacob, see X j.

IX e—Otto, Margarethe, Burchard

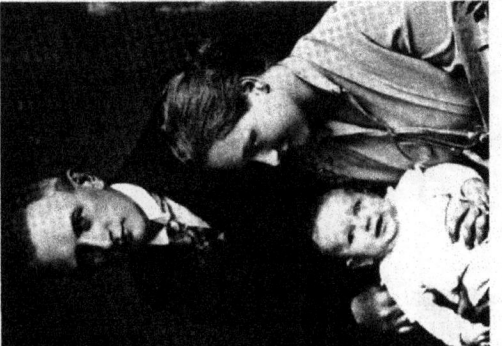

IX e. Otto Johannes, * Neuenkirchen/Oldenburg Nov. 29, 1889, + Norden Feb. 17, 1936, post-office clerk, oo Hagermarsch May 4, 1927 to Margarethe Gerhardine Steffens, * Nordoog June 13, 1907, + Norden Feb. 21, 1962, d.o. Schweer Eppen Steffens, * Nessmerpolder July 7, 1871, + Norden Feb. 3, 1950, farmer, oo Westermarsch April 20, 1906 to Mentje Gerhardine Arens, * Westermarsch Feb. 23, 1887, + Nordoog Aug. 4, 1918.
Children: 1 born in Norden, 2 born in Aurich.
1. Burchard Frerich Otten, see X k.
2. Menna Margarethe Anna, * Nov. 3, 1934, oo Norden March 26, 1960 to Helmut Hermann Kruse, * Norden Nov. 30, 1938, businessman.

—36—

IX f—Werner and Rose

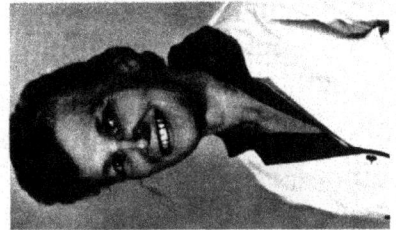 

IX f. Werner Rudolf, * Ostenburg Jan. 14, 1902, farmer, + (missing in action) since April 1945 in USSR, oo Krummin/Usedom April 2, 1930 to Rose Anna Friederieke Athmer, * April 17, 1906, teacher, d.o. Richard Ulrich Athmer, painter and owner of a boarding-house, * Meppen July 21, 1883, + (killed) Verdun, France Aug. 8, 1916, oo Karlshagen/Usedom April 14, 1905 to Emma Amalie Therese Scheeffer, * Nordenburg/Ostpreussen April 27, 1870, + Stralsund May 21, 1945.
Son born in Swinemünde:
1. Hajo, see X l.

—37—

IX g—Otto and Alice

IX g. Otto Theodore Koster, * June 11, 1891, dairy superintendent in Twin Falls, furniture repair specialist in Los Angeles, Calif., + July 26, 1970, oo Dillon, Montana Dec. 28, 1920 to Alice Volenette Dowd, born Pyeatt, * Farmington, New Mexico March 17, 1896, d.o. Samuel Stephan Pyeatt, lumber, * Benton County, Arkansas Jan. 28, 1870, + Esmanola, New Mexico Dec. 21, 1901, oo Astec, New Mexico March 2, 1895 to Clara Elisabeth Phelps, * Picketwire, Colorado April 14, 1874, + Grants Pass, Oregon June 3, 1957.
Son born in Twin Falls.
1. Raymond Theodore, see X m.

IX h. Henrich (Henry) Friedrich Koster, * Minonk, Ill. Sept. 25, 1895, farmer in Genesee, Idaho, oo Genesee, Idaho June 3, 1917 to Hattie Louise Scharnhorst, * Genesee Nov. 23, 1897, d.o. Dedrick Scharnhorst, * Sigourney, Iowa Aug. 23, 1861, farmer at Genesee, + July 5, 1964, oo Genesee Sept. 7, 1890 to Wilhelmina Oldag, * Farmersburg, Iowa Oct. 3, 1874, + Genesee Nov. 28, 1920.
Children: 1 and 2 born in Moscow, Idaho.
1. Betty Louise, * March 20, 1925, oo Genesee, Idaho June 3, 1944 to Philipp O. Greenwell, farmer in Genesee, * Spokane, Washington Aug. 25, 1921.
2. Ralph Eugene, see X n.

IX i—Arthur and Kathryn Koster

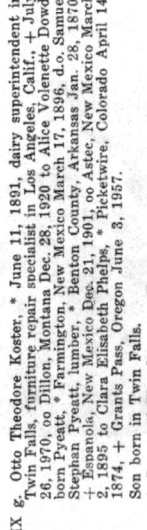

IX i. Arthur Hermann Koster, * Rock Falls, Ill. Oct. 3, 1901, real estate (retired), oo 3 times: a) Idaho Falls, Idaho June 2, 1926 to Delfie Ruth Peterson, * Pilot Mount, Iowa Aug. 9, 1898, + Idaho Falls Feb. 23, 1939, d.o. Gustave Peterson, pastor, * Heda, Ostergotland, Sweden Oct. 29, 1857, + Idaho Falls Aug. 11, 1935, oo April 21, 1891 to Annie Anderson, * Ovidskloster, Skane May 31, 1866 (Sweden), + Idaho Falls March 9, 1954. b) Twin Falls, Idaho June 7, 1941 to Leyla Nelson, * Sherman City March 1, 1905 (Kansas), + Idaho Falls April 13, 1945, d.o. John Franklin Nelson, * Zenia, Indiana Feb. 17, 1863, + Rupert, Idaho Feb. 25, 1938, oo Mount Valley, Kansas Dec. 5, 1895 to Bertha Bell, * Marysville, Kentucky June 4, 1869, + Salem, Oregon July 4, 1944. c) New York City Jan. 17, 1950 to Kathryn Coy, * Timnath, Colorado Dec. 19, 1909, teacher, d.o. James Albert Coy, Grant City, Missouri March 15, 1880, + Mission, Texas March 8, 1958, oo Timnath, Colorado August 8, 1907 to Lida Wilkins, * Timnath Oct 19, 1881, + Idaho Falls June 26, 1952.
Children: (first marriage) 1 and 2 born in Idaho Falls.
1. Roberta Louise, * Aug. 13, 1928, B.S. Whitman College, Walla-Walla, Wash., oo Portland, Oregon Aug. 21, 1954 to Robert Bruce Emerson, * Kimberly, Idaho July 2, 1923, B.S. Idaho State Uni., owners of a drug store.
2. John Earl, see X o.

IX j—Albert and Alma Koster

2. Gertrude Anna, * April 16, 1917, oo Reno, Nevada Oct. 8, 1944 to Harold Sanburn, * Pontiac, Ill. Feb. 19, 1908, mechanical.
3. Roland Alexander, see X q.
4. Mary Jane, * Lakefield May 6, 1923, oo Worthington, Minn. Oct. 31, 1947 to Marvin Washnesky, * Wrenshal, Minn. June 15, 1923, farmer and club manager.
5a. Edith Violet, * Lakefield Nov. 1, 1924, oo Cleveland, Ohio June 12, 1948 to Donald Daykin, * Cleveland, Ohio Feb. 15, 1927, Dr. Mathematician PhD.
  b. Ethel Viola, * Lakefield Nov. 1, 1924, oo Cleveland, Ohio July 28, 1951 to Ferdinand Rodriguez, * Cleveland, Ohio July 8, 1928, Professor on College of Chemical Egineering, "Cornel" Uni.

IX l—Lola, Helen, Albert, Paul

IX l. Albert Paul Koster, * Heron Lake, Minn. Nov. 24, 1900, farmer in Carroll County, Wysop Twp., oo Sterling Dec. 11, 1928 to Helen Margarete Bernadne Eilers, * Sterling May 30, 1908, d.o. Bernhard Eilers, Minsen Friesland Feb. 12, 1865, farmer in Sterling, Sterling Nov. 2, 1928, oo to Hiemke Margarete Elisabeth Hohlen, * Hohenkirchen, Jeverland May 2, 1874, + Sterling July 26, 1930.
Children: 1 and 2 born in Sterling, Illinois.
1. Paul Raymond, see X r.
2. Lola Jeanette, * Sterling Oct. 20, 1931, oo Sterling July 13, 1951 to Richard LeRoy Davis, * Cortland, N.Y. Dec. 7, 1932, carpenter in Sterling.

—41—

IX j. Albert Edward (Bud), * Rock Falls, Ill. Oct. 7, 1907, farmer in Moscow, Idaho, B.S. and M.S. University of Idaho, oo Tacoma, Wash. Oct. 7, 1934 to Alma DeLoris Hodson, * Galena, Kansas April 18, 1914, d.o. Joseph Jessup Hodson, * Quaker Valley, Kansas Sept. 18, 1885, farmer in Galena, Kansas, + Moscow, Idaho Nov. 11, 1961, oo Kamiah, Idaho April 7, 1910 to Eva Hollingsworth, * Quaker Valley, Kansas July 26, 1892.
Children: 1 and 2 born in Moscow, Idaho.
1. Kathleen Marie, * Oct. 2, 1935, B.S. University of Idaho, oo Carmel, Calif. Dec. 29, 1960 to Curtis Welby Thomas, * Stanberry, Mo. May 16, 1935, high school teacher with B.S. Northwest Mo. College.
2. Richard Arthur, see X p.

IX k. Otto Janssen Koster, * Flanagan, Ill. Nov. 25, 1893, farmer in Lakefield, Minn. (retired), oo a) Lakefield Feb. 21, 1915 to Frances Augusta Schuldt, * Rost Twp., Jackson County June 27, 1891, + Lakefield June 18, 1968, d.o. Fritz Schuldt, * Bergen/Rugen Feb. 10, 1850, carriage builder, + Lakefield March 19, 1933, oo to Albertina Groener, * _____ 1856, + Worthington, Nobles County May 28, 1941.
Children: 1-6 born in Lakefield.
1. Margaret Agnes, * Jan. 16, 1916, 2x oo a) Jan. 14, 1941 to Earl Holshauer, Lakefield Jan. 20, 1911, + _____ 1965, b) Mankato Jan. 4, 1957 to Daryl Kunrth, * Nobles County, Worthington Jan. 4, 1928, service station manager and operator specializing in carburetor repair and small engine overhaul.

—40—

IX m—Otto Johannes and Anne Marie Koster

IX m. Otto Johannes, * April 10, 1901, Dr. sc. nat. 1926-1932, assistant agricultural institute in Halle/Saale since 1945, land-counselor and director in Radewitz and Penkun/Pommern, farmer in Lake Mills, Wisc., + Lake Mills May 6, 1969, oo Hanstedt par. Uelzin May 28, 1936 to Anne-Marie Erika Wilhelmine Gertrud Hedwig von Marcard, * Schweidnitz/Schlesien March 11, 1910, d.o. Wilhelm von Marcard, * Hannover Sept. 20, 1866 Oberst a.D. + Bode par. Uelzen Sept. 5, 1940, oo Hannover July 28, 1908 to Clara von Meding, * Barum par. Uelzin Aug. 2, 1877, + Bad Helmstedt June 30, 1931.

Children: 1-5 born in Stettin; 6 born in Penkun; 7 born in Fallingbostel; 8 born in Haggerstown, Maryland.

1. Barbara Erika, * March 9, 1937, B.A. U. of Wisconsin, oo Philadelphia April 20, 1965 to Harry John Romano, * Orange, N. Jersey Nov. 13, 1932, Supt. of schools, Evansville, Wisconsin.
2. Burchard Otto Werner, see X t.
3. Hajo Wilhelm, see X t.
4. Annemarie Regine Eugenie (Hanni), * Sterling April 9, 1941, B.A. U. of Wisconsin, oo Madison Aug. 5, 1965 to Donald Bernard Bednarek, * Berlin, Wisconsin July 31, 1936.
5. Ihno Elimar, * Stettin Dec. 1, 1942, + Walsrode March 25, 1947.
6. Otto Heinrich Matthias, see X u.
7. Friedrich Carl, * Fallingbostel Dec. 13, 1947, + Watertown, Wisc. June 3, 1953.
8. Margarete Dorothe (Nana), * Hagerstown, Maryland Jan. 26, 1952

—42—

IX n—Christine, Hedy, Dagmar, Jacob

IX n. Jacob Werner, * Tyedmerswarfen Oct. 8, 1902, farmer, + Hohenkirchen/Friesland July 12, 1966, oo Bonnin, Pommern Aug. 21, 1941 to Hedy Maria Pora de Varna, * Bonnin June 20, 1923, d.o. Victor Stephan Porak de Varna, * Feb. 2 6, 1897, landholder, + Berlin Nov. 13, 1941, oo Teschendorf/Pommern May 10, 1921 to Hedwig Stein, * ib. Jan. 6, 1901, + Bonnin Aug. 9, 1942.

Children (4): 1 born in Stettin; 2-4 born in Jever.
1. Barbara, * June 17, 1942, + Bevensen June 20, 1948.
2. Christiane Marie, * Jan. 10, 1953.
3. Dagmar Elisabeth, * Sept. 14, 1957.
4. Silvia Marie-Luise, * Feb. 21, 1965.

—43—

X a—Carl, Mark, Jean, James, Mary, Eleanor, Carol, John

X a. Carl Herman Koster, * Sept. 15, 1917, Manager of Product Quality, International Harvester Co, oo Madison, Wisc. June 16, 1940 to Eleanor Julia Vogel, * Madison, Wisc. July 29, 1920, d.o. George Christian Vogel, * Madison, Wisc. Feb. 28, 1894, general Construction Contractor, + Madison, Wisc. Feb. 1, 1968, oo Janesville, Wisc. July 17, 1917 to Erna Sophie Maahs, * Jefferson, Wisc. Nov. 28, 1894.

Children: 1-6 born in Canton, Illinois.
1. John Carl, see XI a.
2. Carol Ellen, * Dec. 4, 1944, oo Canton, Ill. Nov. 5, 1967 to Gary Funk, * Streator, Ill. Feb. 17, 1945, Salesman, Atlantic-Richfield Co.
3. Mary Alice, * Sept. 24, 1949.
4. Jean Marie, * Jan. 22, 1954.
5. James Alan, * March 2, 1956.
6. Mark William, * Aug. 21, 1957.

—45—

IX o—Werner and Ilse

IX o. Werner Rohlf Burchard, * Goldbeck Sept. 15, 1923, Executive Oak-Electronetics Corp., Crystal Lake, Ill., oo Watertown, Wisc. Dec. 26, 1954 to Ilse Anna Else Harder, * Hamburg Sept. 13, 1925, d.o. John Henry Anton Harder, * April 22, 1895, businessman, + Hamburg Oct. 17, 1937, oo Hamburg April 13, 1921 to Margaretha Slama, * Hamburg Oct. 12, 1896, + Hamburg July 27 or 28, 1943.

Children: 1 born in Watertown, 2 born in Waukesha.
1. Irene Margartha, * Sept. 26, 1955
2. John Henry, * Aug. 31, 1957.

—44—

Werner is mentioned on page 103; he died on 4 Jan 2013, and Ilse died on 27 Apr 2010.

X b—Brian, Frieda, Deva Dee, Marna Lee, Bruce, Walter

X b. Walter Fredrick, * Oct. 29, 1919, supt. Northwestern Steel & Wire Co., oo Chapel at Vaughen Gen. Hospital, Chicago Oct. 27, 1945 to Frieda Marie Martin, * Georgetown, Ohio Sept. 13, 1911, d.o. Charles Robert Martin, * Georgetown, Ohio June 17, 1891, farmer in Georgetown, + Georgetown, Ohio Aug. 21, 1958, oo Georgetown, Ohio to Sarah Adeline Wardlow, * Georgetown, Ohio April 8, 1890, + Oct. 1968.

Children: 1-2 in Springfield, Ill., 3-4 in Sterling, Ill.
1a. Bruce Leon, * Oct. 8, 1946.
1b. Brian LeRoy, * Oct. 8, 1946.
3. Deva Dee, * Nov. 10, 1948.
4. Marna Lee, * Feb. 25, 1950.

—46—

X c—David, Elmer, Norman, Alvera, Linda, Sally, Susan

X c. Elmer Louis, * Dec. 13, 1920, farmer in Sterling, oo Tallahasse, Florida May 22, 1943 to Alvera Gantzert, * Moccasin Montana March 25, 1921, d.o. Paul Gantzert, Nelson, Ill. Dec. 9, 1884, + Clinton, Iowa Sept. 3, 1939, oo Dixon, Ill. Feb. 14, 1913 to Lina Heinrich, * Plotzky near Gommern (Magdeburg) Aug. 21, 1894.
Children: 1-5 born in Sterling.
1. Susan Marie, * April 20, 1947, oo Sterling Aug. 28, 1966 to Wayne Peugh, * Sterling Sept. 26, 1947, farmer.
2. Linda Ann, * May 15, 1948.
3. Norman Paul, * March 7, 1951.
4. David Warner, * Oct. 15, 1952.
5. Sally Ann, * Sept. 14, 1956.

—47—

X d—Virginia, Ronald, Ann

X d. Ronald William, * April 18, 1924, farmer in Emerson near Sterling, oo Sterling June 2, 1946 to Virginia Ruth Deets, * Sterling Feb. 15, 1925, d.o. Lester James Deets,* Sterling Feb. 8, 1892, farmer (retired), oo Sterling Dec. 19, 1923 to Irene Margery (M. Irene) Hartmann, * Sterling Nov. 27, 1902.
    1. Ann Irene, * Sterling Feb. 15, 1949, oo Sterling, Ill. April 18, 1970 to William Chalmers Buckler, * Jan. 11, 1947, Rockford, Ill., machine operator, Warner-Lambert Mfg.

—48—

X e—Christine, Arthur, Roger, Steven, Dorothy

X e. Arthur Henry, * Dec. 30, 1920, farmer in Sterling, oo Morrison, Ill. March 2, 1956 to Dorothy Sloot, * Mt. Prospect, Ill. July 14, 1934, d.o. Nick Sloot, *——, Holland May 19, 1890, farmer, + Chicago Oct. 6, 1941, oo Des Plaines, Ill. Aug. 25, 1923 to Emma van Dyke, * Round Grove, Ill. Aug. 1, 1904.
Children: 1-3 born in Morrison, Ill.
    1. Steven Arthur, * April 30, 1959.
    2. Roger Dale, * March 28, 1962.
    3. Christine Ann, * Sept. 18, 1967.

—49—

X f—Russell, Daniel, Margaret, Douglas

X f. Russell Wesley, * April 25, 1926, farmer in Sterling, B.S. 1951 Ill. Economics, oo Erie, Ill. Oct. 4, 1953 to Margaret (Peggy) Ann Dail, * Erie, Ill. Jan. 2, 1931, d.o. Dubert Devere Dail, farmer in Erie, Ill., * Erie, Nov. 14, 1884, oo Morrison, Ill. Feb. 22, 1910 to Emma Matilde Swanson, * Prophetstown Sept. 30, 1886, + Erie, Ill. Sept. 25, 1934.
Children: 1-2 born in Morrison.
1. Daniel Radford, * July 19, 1955.
2. Douglas Dail, * Sept. 7, 1958.

X g—Elizabeth, Gregory, Julia, Merrill

X g. Merrill Theodore, * Dec. 19, 1929, B.S. in Chemistry, Ill. 1951, Dr. of Veterinary Medicine, Colorado State, 1961, Master of Radiology, Colorado State, 1965, Dr. med. vet. in Silverdale, Wash., oo Nov. 23, 1956 to Elizabeth Ann Jakle, * Bowdon, N. Dakota June 25, 1934, d.o. Harold Cornelius Jakle, * Benson, Ill. May 12, 1901, farmer and in road constructing, + Feb. 12, 1953, oo Jamestown, N. Dakota to Martha Ardella Shaver, teacher (retired) living in Silverdale, Wash.
Children: 1-3 born in Fort Collins, Colorado.
1. Gregory Jakle, * March 6, 1958.
2. Ellen Lynn, * July 3, 1960.
3. Julia Ann, * Sept. 10, 1963.

X h—Wesley and Viola

X h. Wesley Hermann, * Dec. 28, 1933, farmer in Sterling, oo Morrison, Ill. Jan. 7, 1955 to Viola Mae Ottens, * Clinton, Iowa April 21, 1929, d.o. Henry C. Ottens, farmer (retired), * Morrison, Ill. April 9, 1903, oo Fulton, Ill. Feb. 4, 1926 to Grace Anna Bonneur, * Morrison, Ill. April 24, 1904.

X i—Mary, Erwin, Lois, LeRoy, Martin, Erwin, Fredrich, Charles

X i. Erwin Edward, * Jan. 22, 1926, farmer in Lyndon, Ill., oo Sterling Dec. 21, 1947 to Lois Marie Rath, * Savanna, Ill. Jan. 1, 1926, d.o. Julius Henry Rath, * Savanna, Ill. July 4, 1886, + ib. May 9, 1947, oo Mosebach, Ill. Jan. 18, 1917 to Mary Schnitzler, * Mt. Carroll March 25, 1894, + Savanna, Ill. Oct. 5, 1963.

Children: 1-6 born in Sterling.
1. Frederick Julius, * Sept. 14, 1948.
2. LeRoy Henry, * Dec. 19, 1949.
3. Erwin Karl, * Sept. 13, 1953.
4. Martin George, * Dec. 11, 1961.
5. Charles Richard, * Feb. 14, 1963.
6. Mary Josephine, * Nov. 5, 1966.

X l—Lawrence, Rowland, Joyce, Teresa, Katherina, Leah

X j. Lawrence, * April 13, 1928, farmer in Harmon, oo Sterling Nov. 26, 1947 to Joyce Rowland, * Sterling Sept. 21, 1929, d.o. LeRoy Rowland, * Polo, Ill, Feb. 12, 1907, + Sterling Dec. 20, 1966, oo Clinton, Iowa June 22, 1927 to Neva Andrews, * Kansas City Kansas March 20, 1907.
Children: 1-4 born in Sterling.
1. Kathrine Ann, * Nov. 4, 1948, oo Sterling Aug. 10, 1968 to Roger Hoffman, * Sterling May 27, 1948, engineer.
2. Teresa Jo, * Oct. 22, 1949.
3. Rowland Lawrence, * Feb. 9, 1955.
4. Leah Marie, * July 5, 1957.

—54—

X k—Burchard, Gretchen, Heidi, Linda

X k. Burchard Frerich Otten, * Feb. 12, 1928, farmer in Sterling, Ill., oo Sterling St. Paul Church Nov. 22, 1953 to Gretchen Taline Luebbers, * Sterling Jan. 4, 1932, d.o. Bernhard Henrikus Luebbers, farmer, * Westerbur Aug. 26, 1904, + Sterling Sept. 16, 1967, oo Sterling Nov. 7, 1931 to Wilhelmine Johanne Michels, * Sande near Wilhelmhaven May 16, 1902.
Children:
1. Heidi Gretchen, * Chicago May 4, 1962.
2. Linda Ann, * Chicago Nov. 25, 1966.

—55—

X l—Torsten, Karsten, Gisela, Hajo, Ingarose

X l. Hajo, * June 13, 1930, Dr. med. vet. in Wilhelmshaven, oo Butzbach/Hessen Aug. 24, 1960, to Gisela Doris Elisabeth Muller, * Breslau/Schlesien Nov. 19, 1936, d.o. Konstantin Karl Muller, * Breslau May 12, 1903, lawyer and notary in Butzbach/Hessen, oo Frankenstein/Oberschlesien Kapelle in Wartha Oct. 8, 1932 to Antonie Martha Tilk, * Frankenstein Sept. 27, 1904.

Children: 1-2 born in Hage/Ostfriesland, 3 born in Wilhelmshaven.
1. Inga Rose Antonie, * Feb. 16, 1961.
2. Torsten Warner Konstantin, * Sept. 6, 1963.
3. Karsten, * Sept. 13, 1967.

—56—

X m—Erik, Kristi, Evelyn, Ted

X m. Raymond Theodore (Ted), * Aug. 12, 1925, furniture repair specialist in Los Angeles, Cal., oo Los Angeles June 14, 1953 to Evelyn Ann Howard, born Bilimek, * Kansas City, Mo. June 29, 1926, d.o. Rudolph Chestine Bilimek, grocery businessman, * St. Joseph, Mo. Oct. 12, 1900, + Los Angeles May 16, 1945, oo June 10, 1922 to Neil Myrtle Pennington, * Frankfort, Kansasas March 18, 1896.

Children: 1-3 born in Los Angeles.
1. Lu Ann, * Sept. 19, 1954, + Los Angeles Dec. 23, 1959.
2. Erik, * July 17, 1962.
3. Kristi Ann, * June 2, 1965.
4. Becky Lee Howard, d.o. Evelyn Ann Howard, * Aug. 24, 1945.

—57—

X 6—John Earl and Joyce Koster

X o. John Earl, * Aug. 9, 1930, B.S. U. of Idaho, insurance broker, oo Brightwaters, Long Island, N.Y. Sept. 9, 1956 to Joyce Prime, * Bay Shore, Long Island, N.Y. Oct. 26, 1933, d.o. William Joseph Prime, * Brooklyn, New York Nov. 20, 1899, oo Woodhaven, New York April 25, 1926 to Alice Marie Hantz, * Woodhaven, N. Y. May 18, 1905. Children: 1 and 2 born in San Rafael, Calif.
  1. Karen Louise, * March 21, 1959.
  2. Nancy Elizabeth, * Nov. 7, 1961.

—59—

X n—Ralph, Susan, Dawn, Scott, Jodell, Michael

X n. Ralph Eugene, * May 2, 1931, auto dealer, B.S. Pacific Lutheran College, oo Genesee April 4, 1954 to Dawn LaVera Heinrich, * Genesee Aug. 27, 1935, d.o. William A. Heinrich, grain farmer in Genesee, * Watertown, S. Dakota Feb. 12, 1896, oo Genesee, Idaho Feb. 21, 1926 to Mary LaVera Daugherty, * North-Powder Feb. 14, 1902. Children: 1, 3, 4 born in Moscow, Idaho, 2 born in Cherry Point, North Carolina.
  1. Michael Craig, * March 15, 1955.
  2. Susan Kae, * March 8, 1956.
  3. Jodelle Dawn, * May 12, 1958.
  4. Scott Ralph, * April 21, 1964.

—58—

X q. Roland Alexander Koster, * March 26, 1919, brick layer, oo Little Rock, Arkansas April 1, 1942 to Betty Blankenburg, * Lakefield Feb. 14, 1924, d.o. August William Blankenburg, * Jackson, A. May 17, 1892, veterinary, oo Jackson County July 23, 1913 to Abbie Beck, Lone Lake, Jackson, Minn. June 22, 1895.
Children: 1-10.
1. Bruce Alexander, see XI b.
2. Gail Janet, * Worthington July 23, 1945, oo Lakefield Dec. 21, 1964 to Lonnie Henry, * Fairmont, Minn. Aug. 18, 1945, works in government.
3. Linda Joy, * Worthington, Minn. Sept. 9, 1948, oo Belmont Jan. 28, 1968 to Lloyd I. Bottin, * Aloha, Minn. Oct. 5, 1945, airforce.
4. Joel Roland, * Worthington April 6, 1951.
5. Jill Ann, * Worthington June 1, 1952.
6. Beth Abbie, * Roseau, Minn. Oct. 25, 1953.
7. Laurel Jean, * Warroad, Minn. Aug. 16, 1956.
8. Julie Lynn, * Lakefield, Minn. March 23, 1959.
9. Lee Allan, * Lakefield May 27, 1960.
10. Shelley Rena, * Lakefield Nov. 2, 1964.

X —Carolyn, Kimberly, Paul, Shauna

X r. Paul Raymond Koster, * June 14, 1929, farmer in Milledgeville, oo Sterling Feb. 1957 to Carolyn Mae Nelson, * Sterling May 17, 1932, d.o. Martin Gordon Nelson, * Chicago May 10, 1910, construction worker, + Sterling June 18, 1960, oo Rock Island Dec. 10, 1932 to Esther Helen Jacobs, * Tampico April 11, 1912.
Children: 1-3 born in Sterling.
1. Sheldon Paul, * + Dec. 17, 1959.
2. Kimberly Pier, * Feb. 2, 1961.
3. Shauna Paige, * Oct. 13, 1964.

—61—

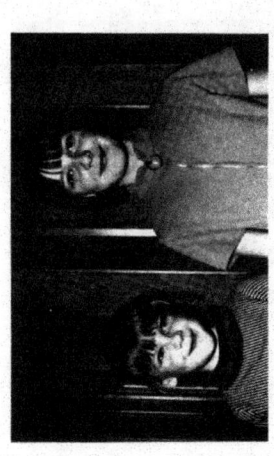

X p—Lisa Rae and Laura Lee

X p. Richard Arthur, * April 3, 1937, farmer in Moscow, B.S. U. of Idaho, oo Moscow, Idaho Sept. 8, 1957 to Patricia Jo Lawton, * Moscow Dec. 2, 1937, B.S. U. of Idaho, d.o. Jackson Howard Lawton, * Spokane, Wash. July 5, 1902, auto dealer, + Moscow April 11, 1956, oo Colfax, Wash. April 12, 1936 to Doris Lula Yarnell, * Oakdale, Wash. Sept. 15, 1918.
Children: 1and 2.
1. Laura Lee, * Fort Eustis, Virginia June 10, 1960.
2. Lisa Rae, * Moscow, Idaho Nov. 13, 1962.

X p—Richard and Patricia Koster

—60—

165

X s. Burchard Otto Werner, * June 30, 1938, farmer and employee, oo Spooner, Wis. June 24, 1967 to Elsa Mae Isabella, * Spooner Feb. 17, 1941, teacher, d.o. Joseph James Isabella, engineer, * Spooner Feb. 6, 1904, oo Rockford, Ill. Dec. 19, 1932 to Vivian Georgette Conrad, * West-Salem, Wis. March 7, 1911.
Children: 1-2.
1. Karla Kay, * Fort Atkinson July 21, 1968.
2. Kurt Joseph, * Fort Atkinson Jan. 31, 1971.

X t—Hajo, Marie and Gregory Koster

X t. Hajo Wilhelm Koster, * Stettin, Germany Nov. 9, 1939, M.S. in Electrical Engineering, oo St. Louis, Mo. June 14, 1969 to Rose Marie Wollmershauser, * St. Louis, Mo. Jan. 26, 1938, d.o. Louis Fred Wollmershauser, * St. Louis, Mo. Jan. 20, 1888, + St. Louis, Mo. Jan. 18, 1962 and Marie Wollmershauser, * Deutsch-Schutzen, Burgenland, Austria Aug. 6, 1897, + St. Louis, Mo. Oct. 29, 1970.
Children: 1.
1. Gregory Hajo, * Washington, D.C. March 14, 1970.

X v—Otto Henrich and Lynn

X v. Otto Heinrich Matthias, * Penkun Dec. 12, 1944, B.A. U. of Wisc. oo Hanstedt, Germany Aug. 15, 1970 to Lynne Yvonne Sanford, * Aug. 31, 1945 in Montgomery, Alabama, B.A. in child psychology, d.o. Gilbert Avery Sanford, sociologist, * May 26, 1910 in New York, oo Mary Elizabeth Gaulding March 13, 1937 in Tifton, Georga, * Feb. 2, 1907.

XI a. John Carl Koster, * April 5, 1941, Service Engineer, Ampex Corp., oo Madison, Wisc., July 17, 1966 to Laura Trujillo, * Giradot, Colombia Sept. 4, 1942, d.o. of Camillo Trujillo, * Neiva, Colombia Oct. 12, 1895, accountant, oo Blanca Borrero, * Neiva, Colombia Sept. 16, 1905.
Children: 1-2 born in Madison, Wisconsin.
1. Monica Ann, * Oct. 28, 1967.
2. Carl Henry, * Aug. 4, 1969.

XI b. Bruce Alexander Koster, * Palm Beach, Florida June 16, 1943, navy, oo Windom, Minn. May 4, 1968 to Marlene Thom. * Windom March 21, 1948, d.o. Raymond Thom, * Ashton, Iowa Feb. 24, 1915, farmer in Windom, oo Adrian, Minn. June 10, 1940 to Viola Berning, * Adrian, Minn. March 8, 1918.
1. Brian Bruce, * Lakefield, Minn. Nov. 10, 1969.

FOURTH (FEDDERWARDER) BRANCH

VII d. Johann Christean Koster, * Gross-Warfen 1-27-1823, + Burg-Knyphausen, cong. Fedderwarden 10-4-1901, farmer, oo twice, a) to Teete Margarethe Heeren, * 11-9-1848, b) to Engeline Harms, * Fedderwarden, + 2-15-1906.

Children: (1st wife) 3-4 born at Fedderwarden.
1. Otto Johannsen, see VIII o.
2. Herman
(Second wife)
3. Johanne, * 12-3-1862, oo Johann Flugel, farmer at Oldorf near Varel.
4. Friederike, * 2-22-1864, oo 4-28-1896 to Reinhard Willms, * Westgaste near Norden 5-12-1864, innkeeper at Waddewarden.

VIII o. Otto Johannsen Koster, * Tammhausen, cong. Oldorf, 11-5-1849, + Breddewarden, con. Sengwarden, 3-11-1880, farmer, oo to Johanne Jhnken, * 2-18-1858, + Wiarden 6-1-1923.

Children born at Breddewarden:
1. Therese, * ___ oo ___ Eisman, at Burgerfelde near Oldenburg.
2. Herman Anton Eduard, see IX s.

IX t. Herman Anton Eduard Koster, * Breddewarden 12-3-1878, buyer at Rustringen, oo Wilhelmshaven 9-9-1905 to Johanne Friedericke Funke, * 1-27-1882.

Daughter born at Rustringen:
1. Johanne Margarethe Elisabeth, * 7-2-1909.

FIFTH (WADDEWARDER) BRANCH

VII e. Burchard Friedrich Koster, * Waddewarden 5-4-1830, + Jever 5-1-1891, farmer at Grosswassens, oo twice, a) to Anke Christine Gerdes, * Canarienhausen, 4-1-1831, + Gross-Wassens 2-10-1866; b) to Metke Marie Meenen, * 4-10-1841, + Jever 5-29-1913.

Children: 1-3 born at Tunnen, 4-9 at Gross-Wassens.
First wife.
1. Otto Gerhard Friedrich, see VIII p.
2. Gerhard Ulrich, see VIII q.
3. Helene Wilhelmine Johanne, * 1-12-1859, + Pophausen 8-18-1924, oo 2-12-1878 to Heinrich Melchior Janssen, * 3-7-1851, + Waddewarden 9-17-1925, butler at Pophausen.
4. Annchen Friederike, * 4-29-1861, oo Adolph Struver, buyer at Berlin, formerly at Hanover.
5. Friedrich Bernhard, see VIII r.
Second wife.
6. Bernhard Julius, * 6-6-1867 + Emerson, Nebr. 1920, farmer.

—64—

7. Marie Henriette, * 12-1-1869, oo Dumfries, Iowa 7-11-1890 to Johann Gerrietz Behrens, * Hookfiel 5-21-1864, farmer at Dumfries, Iowa.
8. Wilhelm Richard, * 1-19-1878, high school custodian at Berlin, oo Gross-Wassens 2-24-1900 to Meta Henriette Cornelius, * Hohewerth, 9-9-1879.
9. Johann Christian, see VIII s.

VIII p. Otto Gerhard Friedrich Koster, * Tunnen 8-17-1853, farmer at Council Bluffs, Iowa.

VIII q. Gerhard Ulrich Koster, * Tunnen 11-27-1855, farmer at Gross-Wassens, oo 4-29-1884 to Gesine Margarete Herzog, * 3-4-1861.

Children born at Bottens:
1. Annchen Margarete, * 10-4-1885, oo Waddewarden 5-16-1908 to Hermann Diedrich Hashagen, * Nordermoor 10-18-1875, teacher at Hoyerswege near Delmenhorst.
2. Gerhard Friedrich, * 6-2-1887, + in battle at Serge, Russia 3-6-1915, Guard-Rgt. no.

VIII r. Friedrich Bernhard Koster, * Gross-Wassens 8-19-1863, buyer at Jever, oo 5-17-1891 to Marie Franzen, * Friedeburg in East Friesland 10-27-1866.

Children born at Jever:
1. Alma Gesine, * 11-22-1891, oo 8-15-1919 to Paul Rabe, * Syke 3-3-1883, at Mulheim (Ruhr).
2. Johann Erich, * 1-6-1893, buyer at Jever.
3. Fritz Gerhard, * 1-30-1895, buyer at Jever.

VIII s. Johann Christian Koster, * Gross-Wassens 1-17-1880, farmer at Cluny, Alberta, Canada, oo Lena Kursteiner, * Bernin in Posen, 11-9-1878.

Children:
1. Hilda, * 1910.
2. Edna, * 1911.
3. Hugo, * 1913.

SIXTH (BLERSUMER) BRANCH

VII f. Hermann Theodor Koster, * Blersum 4-12-1839, + 5-26-1913, wharfsman, oo 4-17-1865 to Rienste Margaretha Theilen, * Cleverns 3-12-1838, + Blersum 9-15-1900.

Children born at Blersum:
1. Otto Johann Hermann, see VIII t.
2. Johanne Marie Catharina, 11-3-1870, + 11-3-1888.

VIII t. Otto Johann Hermann Koster, * Blersum 9-16-1866, + 12-11-1918, wharfsman, oo 11-3-1893 to Tomke Wubkea Margaretha Cordes, * Abens 7-6-1874.

—65—

FUTURE EVENTS

Children born at Biersum:
1. Johanne Marie Christine, * 2-24-1894, oo 10-16-1920 to Johann Wilhelm Beenken, * Feldhausen 5-22-1886, farmer at Abens.
2. Hermann Theodor, * 4-22-1896, farmer at Biersum, oo Wittmund 12-7-1927 to Gesine Reents, * Uflande, Jever 9-10,1897.

SEVENTH (RAHRDUMER) BRANCH

VII g. Folkert Otten Koster, * Biersum 3-21-1845, + Rahrdum near Jever 4-1-1887, oo Memarich Sanders, * Moorhusen near Georgsheil 5-14-1849, oo before to Siebelt Kollmann, —— at Rahrdum.
Children: 1-2 born at Jever, 3-4 at Rahrdum.
1. Otto Janssen, see VIII u.
2. Anna Katharina, * 4-19-1878, + Rahrdum 2-23-1900.
3. Boike Anton, see VIII v.
4. Johannn Hermann, see VIII w.

VIII u. Otto Janssen Koster, * Jever 2-16-1874, inspector at Rahrdum, oo twice, a) Buttforde 11-7-1907 to Anna Bremer, * Heuwarfen near Buttforde 8-12-1882, + Rahrdum 9-27-1916, b) Rahrdum 11-29-1918 to Anna Angelbeck, * Jever 10-6-1894.
Children: 1-3 born at Jever, 4-5 at Rahrdum.
First wife.
1. Folkert Bernhard, * 4-10-1909.
2. Elise Catherine Marie, * 4-27-1910.
3. Heino Martin, * 3-20-1911.
4. Mariechen Adele, * 6-1-1912.
Second wife.
5. Elfriede Ottilie, * 9-2-1920.

VIII v. Boike Anton Koster, * Rahrdum 3-31-1876, farmer at Sterling, Ill., oo twice. a) Katherine Bruns, + Chatsworth, Iowa, b) to her sister Ida Bruns, * 11-30-1894.
Children, 2-3 born at Jever.
First wife.
1. Dorothea Helms, * Chatsworth, Iowa 9-21-1917.
Second wife.
2. Irene, * 5-28-1921.
3. Wilma, * 9-16-1922, + Trouth.
4. Wesley.

VIII w. Johann Hermann Koster, * Rahrdum 11-7-1883, carpenter, oo Reersum near Resterhafe 9-2-1906 to Anna Gerhardine Campen, * 11-17-1883.
Children: 2-6 born at Rahrdum.
1. Marie Aline, * Jever 10-21-1906.
2. Frieda Adele, * Jever 12-15-1907.
3. Gertrude Johanne, * 12-29-1909.
4. Anna Gerhardine, 6 6-21-1911.
5. Johanne Hermine, * 3-10-1912.
6. Erika, * 10-2-1925.

—66—

FUTURE EVENTS

www.ingramcontent.com/pod-product-compliance
Lightning Source LLC
Chambersburg PA
CBHW060532100426
42743CB00009B/1510